MORE FLAVORS

of Myrtle Beach, South Carolina

A COOKBOOK FEATURING FAVORITE RESTAURANT RECIPES

(FEB. 20 - 001)

COMPILED AND WRITTEN BY DENISE MULLEN

**Published by The Sun News
of Myrtle Beach, South Carolina**

First printed in May 1998. Printed in the United States of America

ISBN 0-9625035-3-3

Project Director: Jody Hazzard

Cover photograph: Charles Slate

Front and back cover design: Jacque Carter

Editorial: Denise Mullen

Book design and editing: Jody Hazzard

Copy editors: Steven J. Smith, Barbara Horner and
              Sharon Eagles-McCants

On the cover, clockwise from top left: The Charleston Cafe's Scratch Bloody Mary Mix (recipe on page 30); The Mayor's House Restaurant's Milky Way Cheesecake (recipe on page 69); Thoroughbreds' Restaurant's French Onion Soup (recipe on page 123); Thoroughbreds' Restaurant's Grilled Portabello Mushrooms (recipe on page 122); Sea Captain's House's Crab Cakes with Lemon Dill Butter Sauce (recipe on page 111); The Olive Garden's Grilled Swordfish Pomodoro and Capellini Pomodoro (recipes on page 86); and Sea Captain's House's Shrimp Salad (recipe on page 112).

Additional copies of "More Flavors of Myrtle Beach, South Carolina" may be obtained by mailing a check for $12.95 to More Flavors of Myrtle Beach, The Sun News, Attn. Cashier, P.O. Box 406, Myrtle Beach, S.C. 29578. Price includes postage and handling. S.C. residents add 50¢ for sales tax. Make checks payable to The Sun News. Or call our customer service department at 1-800-568-1800.

A specialty publication of

THE SUN NEWS
WHERE YOU GO TO KNOW.

http://www.myrtlebeachaccess.com

Table of Contents

Introduction

There is one question that is invariably asked by both the hundreds of thousands of visitors to the Grand Strand each year and area locals: "Where's a good place to eat?"

That is the one important question that "More Flavors of Myrtle Beach, South Carolina" strives to answer with honesty and flair. And, it's no easy task when you consider that this 60-mile stretch of coastline is home to upwards of 1,800 dining establishments. The Grand Strand has the distinction of offering more restaurants per capita than San Francisco! Yet, this incredible number of eating venues seems undaunting to the industry as our ravenous public is treated to more new tables every year.

To South Carolinians, this region is known as the Lowcountry. It's the land kissed by sun and surf. It's more fun and shopping than one can experience in one week's vacation. It's the best eating around.

Certain Grand Strand locales immediately summon tastebuds to the flavors of freshly caught seafood, expertly prepared. Those areas include Little River and Murrells Inlet. There's an area just north of Myrtle Beach named Restaurant Row, since this strip was built up around long-standing, exceptional eateries. Almost anything worth noshing can be found along the Grand Strand from French, Italian and Continental cuisines to Mexican, Japanese and Chinese.

This recipe book has been published by Myrtle Beach's local daily newspaper, The Sun News, in an attempt to bring the best of Grand Strand food to your kitchen. Since the restaurant industry itself is so viable to the economic well-being of the Grand Strand, The Sun News is committed to keeping up-to-date on its current scene. This information is important to the communities served by the newspaper. Conversely, it's just as important to our visitors.

As we did with our first book, "Flavors of Myrtle Beach, South

Carolina," we have sifted through the current players on the restaurant scene to present a credible cross-section of some of the best dining in town. In "More Flavors of Myrtle Beach, South Carolina," you'll find, like we have, that really good food can be found in some of the most unlikely places and taste sensations can arise from a most curious marriage of ingredients.

In a region with so many dining establishments, it stands to reason that favorite recipes are critical to reputation and repeat business. Competition is fierce and restaurants usually guard their most-ordered dishes. In other cases, food preparation is tied to family heritage and allowing a recipe to be widely distributed is tantamount to publishing a family member's diary. For all of these reasons, we extend heartfelt gratitude to the restaurants included in "More Flavors of Myrtle Beach, South Carolina," that have so unselfishly given to the publication of this book.

The selection process for this book was an arduous one. An independent survey poll was conducted to narrow down the restaurants that would be the most interesting experiences for cultivated diners and cooks, alike. Unfortunately, in some cases, a selected establishment was not able to participate due to time constraints or confidentiality of recipes.

The recipes printed in this cookbook have been submitted by the restaurant manager and/or chefs and were all doublechecked and proofed a second time by the restaurant personnel.

The following pages contain brief descriptions of the restaurants, followed by several mouth-watering recipes. We've also included maps in the back of the book to help you find the restaurants, a helpful glossary of terms, plus an index to help you find recipes by categories.

All in all, we are sure that this cookbook will impart to you valuable information about the Grand Strand restaurant scene and have you cooking up a storm once you've recreated and tasted one of these delectable dishes.

For more information on dining in the Myrtle Beach area, check out The Sun News in cyberspace at http://www.myrtlebeachaccess.com

Anchovies Restaurant

4079 U.S. 17 Business
Murrells Inlet
(843) 651-0664

Anchovies not only serves up great fresh food, it also treats diners to a panoramic view of swaying grasses amid a natural saltmarsh. At viewing vantage from the dining room, screened porch or waterfront deck, the effect is nearly hypnotic. You're sure to feel relaxed, hungry and comfortable at this waterfront establishment.

The casual ambience is also pointed up by lots of natural light, wood floors, booth seating and the invitation of the central bar. Anchovies' menu is eclectic. The restaurant's name implies a seafood house, but mouthwatering Italian dishes (including pizza), steaks and such appetizers as baked mozzarella with marinara sauce are just as popular here.

Plan to dress down, sidle up to the bar for a couple of pre-dinner cocktails and then mosey on over to a table to enjoy a superb meal with the sounds of the marsh as a perfect backdrop.

Pina Colada Cheesecake

1⅔ cups dry breadcrumbs
¼ cup sugar
½ cup butter, melted
4 8-ounce packages of cream cheese
¾ cup sugar
4 large eggs
1 8-ounce carton sour cream
1 16-ounce can cream of coconut
1 15-ounce can crushed pineapple, drained
2 tablespoons cornstarch
1 teaspoon vanilla
1 teaspoon rum flavoring
1 teaspoon lemon juice

For Topping:
¼ cup butter
½ cup flaked coconut
½ cup almonds, finely chopped
¼ cup sugar

To make the crust, combine the first 3 ingredients and press into the bottom and one inch up the sides of a 10-inch springform pan. Bake at 350 degrees for 10 to 12 minutes. Cool on a rack.

Beat cream cheese at medium speed until smooth. Gradually add in the ¾ cup of sugar beating well. Add the eggs, one at a time, beating well after each. Stir in the sour cream and next 6 ingredients.

Spoon into the crust. Bake at 350 degrees for one hour and 20 minutes. Turn off the oven. Take out the cheesecake and sprinkle on the topping (instructions follow). Return to the oven and leave there with the door closed for one hour. Take the finished cheesecake out and cool on a rack. Chill in the refrigerator before cutting. Garnish with a fresh slice of lime if you like. Serves 10 to 12 people.

To prepare the topping, melt ¼ cup of butter in a sauté pan. Add in the flaked coconut, chopped almonds and ¼ cup of sugar and, stirring frequently, cook until golden brown in color.

Fisherman's Pasta

- 12 scallops (30-40 count)
- 14 medium shrimp
- 2   ounces lump crabmeat
- ½   cup butter
- ½   quart heavy cream
- ¼   cup Parmesan cheese, grated
- 12 ounces fettuccini, cooked al dente
- Salt and pepper to taste

Melt the butter in a skillet. Add the scallops and shrimp and sauté for about 2 minutes over medium heat. Stir in the crabmeat and heavy cream and cook until the mixture is reduced and becomes slightly thickened.

Remove from heat and add the Parmesan cheese, salt and pepper. Mix well and pour over cooked pasta. Garnish with a lemon wedge and finely chopped parsley if desired. Makes 2 dishes.

Lowcountry Grouper

- 2   8-ounce grouper filets
- 1   cup flour
- 1   cup butter
- 4   ounces mushrooms, sliced
- 1   large shallot, chopped
- 3   cloves garlic, chopped
- 1   cup dry white wine

Dredge grouper in the flour and sauté in ½ cup of melted butter for 3 minutes on each side, over medium heat. Pour butter off, add wine, shallots and mushrooms and simmer for about 3 minutes.

Next, add the chopped garlic and another ½ cup of butter and cook for another one to two minutes, or until done to your liking.

Place the prepared filet on a serving dish and pour the sauce over top. Garnish with lemon slices if you so desire. Serves 2.

Austin's
At The Beach

2606 N. Kings Highway
Myrtle Beach
(843) 448-9058

Once a stately private home, Austin's is a favorite for locals who enjoy fine dining and wonderful lunch specials. Even though owners Bill and Annette Austin don't expect their patrons to dress up to dine here, the tables are always adorned with candles and fresh flowers.

Bill Austin is the head chef who graduated with honors from The Culinary Institute of America and has delighted customers with his personal twist on traditional preferences like rack of lamb and filet mignon. Always experimenting to find a more interesting taste for sauces and food preparation, Austin's has placed first many times at the annual Taste of the Town competition.

The fare at Austin's is described as "gourmet contemporary American" with fare like herb crusted salmon with a Dijon mustard and clover honey glaze, pecan crusted Carolina blue crab cakes and Oysters Orleans.

Austin's Chocolate Fudge Nut Pie

4	ounces chocolate, chopped
4	ounces butter
1½	cups granulated sugar
1	cup packed brown sugar (dark or light)
1	cup heavy cream
½	cup Karo syrup (light)
2	teaspoons vanilla extract
½	teaspoon salt
6	eggs
3	cups chopped nuts (pecans or walnuts are best)
2	9-inch chocolate crumb pie crusts

Melt the chocolate and butter in a double boiler. Add everything else but the nuts and whisk together. Fold in the nuts and pour into the crust. Bake at 350 degrees for 45 to 55 minutes. Makes 2 pies. Apparently, one is never enough!

BENITO'S

Benito's Brick Oven and Ristorante Italiano

1308 Celebrity Circle
Broadway at the Beach
Myrtle Beach
(843) 626-8184

Benito's represents two restaurants, standing side by side, in the middle of the busy Broadway At The Beach complex. Diners can choose a relaxed booth at the brick oven locale or a table decked out in linen at the ristorante. Whether you choose door number one or door number two, you're in for an Italian taste treat that traverses 70 regional wines, specialty pizzas, fascinating pasta combinations (the penne alla vodka is to-die-for) and gourmet dishes.

Everything served by the hands of Benito's is made to order and fresh. Take their antipasto salad for two, for example: It's a bed of crisp lettuce, heaped with chunks of chicken pesto, rich ribbons of roasted red peppers, bite-sized pieces of breaded eggplant, circles of black olives and perfect squares of mozzarella cheese.

The original Benito's is only five years old and seemed to catch on right away as hungry patrons flocked there to eat such yummies as a hand-tossed ricotta cheese pizza, hot stromboli or homemade chicken cacciatore. The younger, ristorante is only a year old, giving chef Frank Letino the perfect kitchen in which to flex his culinary muscles. Benito's Ristorante Italiano also coordinates regular wine tasting evenings.

Deli Stromboli

1	package active dry yeast
½	cup warm water
1	teaspoon salt
1	teaspoon sugar
4	cups flour
2	cups mozzarella cheese
1	cup ham, diced
1	cup salami
1	cup pepperoni

Dissolve the yeast in the warm water. Combine the salt, sugar and flour in a mixing bowl. Add in the yeast and begin mixing, adding small amounts of extra water as needed until the dough begins to hold together. Mix for 7-10 minutes, then cover and set aside until the dough doubles in bulk, about one hour.

Punch the dough down and cut into four equal portions. Using a rolling pin, flatten each portion into a 10-inch by 6-inch rectangle.

Add equal amounts of Mozzarella cheese and meats to each, then fold the dough upwards and press it together over the top of the filling. Fold the edges in and press together.

Place on a pizza stone or cookie sheet and bake in a preheated 375-degree oven until golden brown, about 30 minutes. Makes 4 strombolis.

Sausage Contadina

1½	pounds Italian sausage
4	tablespoons olive oil
4	cloves garlic, chopped
1	small onion, diced
1	cup mushrooms, sliced
1	cup white wine
2	cups tomato sauce
2	tablespoons fresh basil, chopped
2	pounds rigatoni, cooked

Salt and pepper to taste

Cook the sausage in a 375-degree oven for about 45 minutes. When cool enough, cut into 1-inch pieces.

Heat the olive oil and garlic in a pan. Add in the onion and mushrooms and allow to cook. Then add the sausage and wine and simmer for 2 minutes. When ready to serve, add the tomato sauce and basil, heat thoroughly, salt and pepper to taste and pour over the rigatoni. Makes 4 servings.

Pollo Alla Scarpariello

4	tablespoons olive oil
4	chicken breasts
	Flour for dredging
1	cup green peppers
1	cup onion
1	tablespoon crushed red pepper
1	cup tomato, diced
2	tablespoons fresh basil, chopped
1	cup marinara sauce

Cut each chicken breast in half and trim the fat. Dredge the chicken in flour and place in the oil that has been heating in a pan. Cook each side for about 2 minutes.

Add the green peppers, onion and red pepper. When everything is cooked, remove the chicken and place on a serving tray. Add the fresh tomato, basil and marinara to the pan. Heat thoroughly and pour over top of the chicken. Garnish with fresh chopped parsley if you like. Makes 4 servings.

Funghetti Aglio e Olio

4	tablespoons olive oil
25-30	small porcini mushrooms
1	teaspoon garlic
4	tablespoons breadcrumbs
1	teaspoon fresh parsley, chopped
	Romano cheese for garnish
	Salt and pepper to taste

Heat the oil in a non-stick pan. Add the mushrooms and allow to cook, stirring often. Add the garlic after about 2 minutes.

Remove from the heat and sprinkle the remaining ingredients over the mushrooms. Garnish with grated Romano cheese. Serves 6 as an appetizer or side dish.

Shrimp and Chicken Alla Benito

4	tablespoons olive oil
1	tablespoon garlic, chopped
2	chicken breasts
16	shrimp
1	cup pesto sauce
4	cups marinara sauce
1	tablespoon fresh basil, chopped
1	tablespoon fresh parsley, chopped
2	pounds rigatoni, cooked

Flour for dredging
Salt and pepper to taste

Slice the chicken breasts into ½-inch strips (you should end up with about 16 strips). Dredge the strips in flour and cook in a pan with the olive oil and garlic.

Add the shrimp and pesto sauce and let simmer. Cast in the remaining ingredients and toss in a large bowl with the cooked pasta. Makes 4 servings.

Shrimp Fra Diavolo

4	tablespoons olive oil
1	tablespoon garlic, chopped
28	shrimp
1	teaspoon crushed red pepper
8	cups marinara sauce
2	pounds linguine, cooked

Heat the oil and garlic in a frying pan. Toss in the shrimp and red pepper and allow to cook, turning occasionally. When the shrimp are cooked (they turn pink and curl), remove from the heat and stir in the marinara sauce. Pour over the top of cooked linguine in a large pasta bowl. Serves 4.

The Bistro

5101 N. Kings Highway
Myrtle Beach
(843) 449-5125

The Bistro is one of the places that serves its guests character –
in every sense of the word. It began as a small cafe inside the
Parasol Hotel that seemed to be decorated in "early attic" with an
extensive wine collection secured by a wrought-iron gate. All of
this appeared to be held together by a continuous thread of white
twinkling lights. Presented with the opportunity to grow and have
much-needed parking space, the Bistro packed up its stuff and
headed down the road to a new location. It's now a little larger
and includes a New York-style pub.

Cozy and laissez-faire in atmosphere, the cast and crew of The
Bistro is made up of waiters who bear their own distinct
personalities, which are worn as casually as their clothing.

Caesar salad is always prepared tableside at The Bistro. The
menu of continental cuisine stretches from Deutsche
Hausmannskost to Schnitzel to linguine to Greek salad. Local
residents clamor for the specialties of the house, which include an
escargot pasta dish and scrod, pan-sautéed in Japanese breadcrumbs
with a sweet glaze. And a visit to The Bistro would not be complete
without dessert – enjoy an Old English trifle or the raspberries in
cognac.

Boston Scrod

1   8-ounce Canadian cod filet
Clarified butter or margarine for cooking
1   egg
Flour for dredging
Japanese breadcrumbs for coating

Heat the clarified butter or margarine in a sauté pan. Dredge the cod in the flour, and the eggwash and finally, roll it in the Japanese breadcrumbs.

Place the fish in heated clarified butter and brown for approximately 3 minutes. Carefully turn the filet and allow it to cook further until it is completely browned. Remove and serve with homemade tartar sauce and coleslaw (recipes follow). Makes 1 dish.

Bistro Slaw

1   pound cabbage
1   large carrot
¼   cup sweet pickle relish
1   onion
½   cup mayonnaise
Lemon juice to taste

In a food processor, grate cabbage, carrots and onion. Place in a mixing bowl and add the remaining ingredients and lemon juice to taste.

Tartar Sauce

½   cup mayonnaise
2   tablespoons sweet pickle relish
1   onion
Lemon juice to taste

In a serving bowl, mix all of the ingredients together and add lemon juice to taste.

Bovine's

**U.S. 17 Business South
(On the Waterfront)
Murrells Inlet
(843) 651-2888**

Straying – or should we say grazing – from the usual seafood fare of historic Murrells Inlet, Bovine's took to the Southwest, offering a delightfully surprising menu that could only be described as eclectic.

Picture-perfect windows gaze onto a lazy, Lowcountry marsh while the Bovine decor accents the West with cowhide-covered seats, a mounted head of a once huge bull and a wood-fired adobe oven.

With a background in contemporary Southwestern and Caribbean cuisine, nearly every selection on Bovine's menu has an unusual bent. Seafood and aged beef are grilled over mesquite and honey-crusted pizza emerges piping hot from the adobe oven. Desserts run the gamut from Italian tortes to a homemade apple ligonberry cake.

Shrimp and Roasted Corn Fritters with Jalapeno-Honey Tartar

        2   eggs
        ¾   cup milk
        2½   cups sifted flour
        1   tablespoon baking powder
        ¾   teaspoon salt
        ¼   cup red onion, chopped
        ¼   cup red pepper, chopped
        2   jalapeno peppers, chopped
        1   cup roasted corn
        1½   cups cooked shrimp, coarsely chopped
        6   ounces beer

Beat eggs and milk together. Add in flour, baking powder, salt, vegetables and beer. Fold in shrimp. Drop approximately 2 tablespoons of the batter into 350-degree oil and fry for 3 to 5 minutes or until golden brown.

Drain on paper towels and serve with Jalapeno-Honey Tartar (recipe follows) and fresh wedges of lemon and lime.

Jalapeno-Honey Tartar

        2   cups mayonnaise
        ¼   cup Dijon mustard
        ¼   cup jalapeno peppers, chopped and seeded
        ¼   cup cilantro, chopped
        ¼   cup dill relish
        ½   cup green onions, chopped
        ½   cup honey

Mix all ingredients together well and chill.

Corn Tortilla Crusted Grouper with Tropical Fruit Salsa

        4   8-ounce grouper filets
        2   cups crushed tortilla chips (food processor works best)
        ½   tablespoon cumin
        2   cups flour
        3   eggs, beaten
        ¼   cup oil
        1 teaspoon each of salt, pepper and garlic
        Juice of 1 lime

19

Dust fish with flour, salt and pepper. Dredge dusted filets in beaten eggs. Mix cumin, salt, pepper, garlic and lime juice with crushed chips. Press the crushed tortilla chips mixture onto filets. Sauté filets in oil for 2 to 3 minutes on each side, in an ovenproof pan. Place pan of fish in a 350-degree oven for 7 to 8 minutes. Serve with Tropical Fruit Salsa (recipe follows).

Tropical Fruit Salsa

1	jalapeno pepper, diced
2	mangos, diced
1	papaya, diced
1	red onion, diced
1	bunch cilantro, chopped
2	limes
1	teaspoon garlic
2	tablespoons olive oil

Salt and pepper to taste

Combine all ingredients, except limes. Serve salsa with fresh lime slices.

Banana Cheesecake with Peanut Butter Sauce

½	pound cream cheese
4	eggs
1	cup sugar
1	teaspoon banana flavoring
2	bananas, mashed
1	Oreo cookie pie crust
1	tablespoon dark rum

Blend cream cheese and sugar together. Add eggs, one at a time, until incorporated. Add flavoring, bananas and rum, mixing well. Pour this batter into pie crust and bake at 300 degrees for one hour. Turn oven off and leave cake in for 15 minutes more. Remove from oven and let cool for 3 to 4 hours. Slice and serve with peanut butter sauce (recipe follows).

Peanut Butter Sauce

1	cup peanut butter
½	cup milk

Bring milk and peanut butter to a simmer on low heat. Remove from heat and let stand for 10 minutes.

Cappuccino's

1535 U.S. 17 North
Little River
(843) 280-8999

Obvious by its name, this cafe is centered around the universal love of coffee. Cappuccino's is decorated in coffee, serves an extraordinary variety of the hot drink and smells heavenly of freshly ground beans.

This is a family-owned-and-operated business, that in one short year of operation has become known for its unique concepts and great luncheon specials. The Morgan clan turns coffee into delectable desserts and even into a specialty martini. Cappuccino's is the first restaurant to offer a make-your-own-Bloody-Mary bar on Sundays during its brunch buffet, which features eggs benedict with jumbo crab cakes instead of Canadian bacon and seafood crepes.

Specials change daily, but always include two pasta dishes (one with a red sauce and the other with a creme version), open-face sandwiches on bakery bread and a fresh seafood dish.

Cappuccino's Stuffed Shrimp

6	jumbo shrimp, peeled, deveined and split
1	green pepper, diced fine
1	red pepper, diced fine
1	large green onion, diced fine
2	cups breadcrumbs (preferably Japanese)
6	slices bacon
½	cup water

Feta cheese

Mix together the peppers and onions and add in the breadcrumbs. Mix to a tight consistency using about ½ cup of water. Roll the feta cheese into 6 balls, each about the size of a quarter. Pat stuffing around the feta, put shrimp around them and wrap tightly with a slice of bacon. Place on a cookie sheet and bake at 350 degrees for about 25 minutes or until the bacon is browned.

Broccoli and Cheddar Soup

1	stick butter
1	large yellow onion, diced fine

Flour, sifted

1	quart rich chicken stock
2	large bunches broccoli, washed and cleaned
2	pounds cheddar cheese, shredded
2	cups 40% heavy cream

Melt the butter in a large saucepan. Add onions and sauté. Make a roux by slowly adding sifted flour, stirring constantly until the consistency is that of paste. Cook until the paste is brown and has a peanut smell. Then, slowly whisk in the chicken stock until the liquid is smooth with no lumps.

Meanwhile, boil the cleaned broccoli until tender in a separate pot. Drain, reserving the liquid, and dice into small pieces. Then, place the cut broccoli back into the water and boil again.

With a whisk, slowly add the roux to the boiling broccoli, stirring constantly. Bring back to a boil and it should thicken. Turn down the heat and add in the cheese and heavy cream until the cheddar melts. Let simmer on low for 15 to 20 minutes.

Kahlua Ice Cream Pie

2   ready-made Oreo cookie pie crusts
1   cup Kahlua
1   cup strong coffee or 2 shots espresso
2   pints coffee ice cream
4-6 Oreo cookies, crumbled
½   cup chocolate chips
Strawberries, chocolate sauce, whipped cream and mint to garnish

Heat Kahlua and coffee in a small saucepan on medium heat until the alcohol has cooked out. Let cool to room temperature, or cool in the refrigerator.

In a large bowl, mix the ice cream, cooled Kahlua, crumbled Oreos and chocolate chips. Fill each pie shell to the top and put in a freezer for at least 3 hours, preferably overnight.

To serve, pour about 2 tablespoons of Kahlua on the bottom of a serving dish. Garnish with strawberries, chocolate sauce, whipped cream and a sprig of mint. Makes 2 pies.

Capt. Dave's
Dockside Restaurant

4037 U.S. 17 Business
Murrells Inlet
(843) 651-5850

Owned and operated by the Owens family for 25 years, you can't hope for a better recommendation than a Southern Living magazine critique that stated, "You could point at the menu with your eyes closed and be assured of a culinary treat." Capt. Dave's is an annual award winner at the Taste of the Tidelands competition and festival for its exceptional cuisine.

The waterfront dining room and deck puts you at the shores of Murrells Inlet and a central fireplace is always crackling on chilly evenings. With its roots tightly linked to these waters, Capt. Dave's is known locally for its fresh seafood, expertly prepared and presented.

This dockside restaurant offers patrons an extensive wine list and good old-fashioned Southern hospitality.

Blackened Triggerfish

(Over stone ground grits, topped with poached oysters in a garlic herb butter)

For the garlic butter:

1	pound butter (at room temperature)
1	tablespoon garlic, chopped
1	tablespoon chives, chopped
1	shallot, chopped
1	tablespoon parsley, chopped
⅛	cup white wine
1	lemon, juiced
½	ounce Pernod or anisette

Mix all these ingredients together in a mixing bowl and refrigerate.

Blackening Seasoning:

2½	teaspoons salt
¾	teaspoon white pepper
1	teaspoon crushed red pepper
¾	teaspoon black pepper
1	tablespoon paprika
1	teaspoon garlic powder
1	teaspoon onion powder
½	teaspoon dry thyme
½	teaspoon dry oregano

Mix all ingredients thoroughly and set aside.

Stone Ground Grits:

1	cup stone ground grits
3	cups water
1	cup milk
½	pound butter
1	tablespoon cracked black pepper
2	teaspoons garlic, minced

Salt to taste

Bring water, garlic, salt, cracked pepper and butter to a boil. Stir in the grits and reduce heat to medium. When thick, add milk and stir. Let simmer for 30 minutes.

Seafood Preparation:
4   6-8 ounce triggerfish filets
½   cup butter, melted
16   fresh oysters, removed from shells

ALERT: Blacken only outside or in a well-ventilated area. Using a black iron skillet, heat to as hot as possible. Dredge triggerfish through the melted butter and then sprinkle with the blackening seasoning to your taste.

Carefully place filets into the hot pan and cook for 3 minutes on each side. Expect the skillet to smoke profusely.

Melt the garlic-herb butter in a sauté pan. When completely liquefied, add the oysters and cook just until they begin to curl.

Place 4 to 5 ounces of grits on each plate. Top the grits with one blackened filet. Arrange 4 oysters over the triggerfish and drizzle more garlic-herb butter overtop. Makes 4 dinners.

Mixed Green Mesculin Salad
(With roasted red pepper and black-eye pea vinaigrette and a baked bleu cheese crouton)
¼   cup black-eye peas
2   ounces fat back
4   cups water
1   red pepper
1¼   cups olive oil
½   cup balsamic vinegar
1   garlic bulb (peeled)
¼   cup Parmesan cheese
¼   cup bleu cheese
6   slices bread, crust removed
Baby organic greens for 6 servings
Salt and pepper to taste

To prepare the peas, brown the fat back in a small saucepan and drain off grease. Add in 4 cups of water and bring to a boil. Reduce heat and simmer for 15 minutes. Pour in the dried peas and cook for 2 hours, adding water as needed. When peas are cooked, strain off the water and reserve. Rinse the peas to cool. Set aside.

For the dressing, blacken the skin of the red pepper by placing it on a grill or under a broiler. When completely blackened, place the pepper in a bowl, cover with plastic wrap and let steam for 15 minutes. Under running water, peel the skin from the pepper, split and remove the seeds. In a food processor, puree the roasted pepper, garlic, vinegar and ¼ cup of the liquid from the peas. When complete, drizzle in one cup of the olive oil. Place all of this in a mixing bowl and add in the peas. Salt and pepper to taste.

To make the croutons, combine ¼ cup of olive oil and the bleu cheese in a small pan and heat until the cheese melts. Spoon the cheese mixture over the slices of bread and bake in a 350-degree oven for 3 minutes.

In a large bowl, toss the organic greens with the pea dressing. Place on individual salad plates, sprinkle with Parmesan cheese and serve with a hot bleu cheese crouton. Makes 6 salads.

Fresh Berries with White Chocolate Creme Anglais and Half Whipped Cream

- 1 pint blackberries
- 1 pint blueberries
- 1 pint strawberries
- 1 quart plus 1 pint heavy whipping cream
- ½ cup sugar
- 8 egg yolks
- 4 ounces white chocolate, diced
- 1 teaspoon pure vanilla

To make the Creme Anglais, take a large mixing bowl and blend together egg yolks and sugar. Whip until pale and then add the white chocolate.

In a small pot, bring 1 quart of whipping cream to a boil while frequently stirring the egg and sugar mixture. Pour half of the hot cream over the egg mixture, stirring well. Pour all of this back into the pot and on the stove over low heat. Continue stirring sauce just until it coats the back of a spoon. Let cool to room temperature and refrigerate overnight.

Prepare the half whipped cream by mixing one pint of whipping cream and sugar to desired sweetness in a mixing bowl. Using an electric mixer, blend on high speed to a medium thickness. Add the vanilla and whip for just 15 seconds to incorporate the ingredients. On a large plate, spoon or ladle 3 ounces of creme anglais. Mix the berries and put them over top the creme anglais and top with the half-whipped cream. Serves 4.

27

The Charleston Cafe

815 Surfside Drive
Surfside Beach
(843) 238-2200

Auspicious in its beginnings, The Charleston Cafe opened its doors to the howling winds of Hurricane Hugo in September 1989. The first week of business found owner and chef David Heckman wandering around in the dark with a flashlight assessing damage, restocking the kitchen with his insurance agent at his side to sign checks and grilling any unspoiled food to give to those in need.

The small, 54-seat cafe has come a long way since that day and now finds itself working hard to accommodate a steady stream of reservations. Heckman attributes the restaurant's success to his regular clientele who "keep me innovative and honest . . . you mustn't bore your diners." The menu is based on "creative preparation of normal ingredients" and Charleston Cafe offers special dishes every evening to keep palates excited.

Heckman says that he'll leave cooking fads to major centers like New York and San Francisco, because he doesn't like wasting time looking for obscure foods. As he so aptly explains, "What's the point in spending time and money looking for a truffle slicer only to have it bronzed when truffles go out of season and out of vogue?"

Along with delicious food, Charleston Cafe has a large by-the-glass wine menu.

Reuben Casserole

- 12 eggs
- 1 cup milk
- 1 loaf day old, seeded rye bread, cut into 1-inch cubes
- 1 cup celery, roughly chopped
- 1 cup carrots, roughly chopped
- 1 cup onions, roughly chopped
- ¼ cup vegetable oil
- 2 cups pastrami, cut into cubes
- 2 cups corned beef, cut into cubes
- 1½ teaspoons ground pepper
- 1½ tablespoons creamed horseradish
- 2 cans sauerkraut, drained
- 2 cups Thousand Island dressing
- 12 thick slices of Swiss cheese

Beat eggs and milk until frothy. Soak rye bread cubes in the egg mixture overnight in the refrigerator.

Sauté vegetables in oil just until soft. Let them cool. When cooled, add to the bread mixture. Then add in the cubed meat, pepper, horseradish and sauerkraut. Toss well to combine all of the ingredients. Press this mixture into a 9X12 greased baking pan.

Spread one cup of the Thousand Island dressing over the pan. Top this with Swiss cheese slices. Spread another cup of Thousand Island dressing over the cheese.

Cover with aluminum foil and bake at 350 degrees until bubbly. Serve with a fresh green salad and bottle of Gewürztraminer or Riesling.

Clara Ryder's Baked Potato Salad

- 1 cup hot water
- 3 bouillon cubes, crushed
- 3 tablespoons minced onion
- 2 tablespoons minced garlic
- ¼ cup olive oil
- 2 tablespoons tarragon leaves, crushed
- ⅛ teaspoon black pepper
- 3 pounds new potatoes, cut into bite-sized pieces

Combine all ingredients, except the potatoes, mixing well. Turn the mixture into a baking pan and then add the potatoes. Turn the potatoes in the mixture to coat well.

Bake, uncovered, in a 350-degree oven for one hour, stirring every 15 minutes. Serve hot, cold or at room temperature.

Scratch Bloody Mary Mix (pictured on the cover)

3	seeded bell peppers, diced fine
3	seeded jalapeno peppers, diced fine
3	bunches green onions, diced fine
1	bunch cilantro, stems removed, diced fine
½	cup minced fresh garlic
½	cup coarsely ground black pepper
1	tablespoon celery seed
1½	cups Worcestershire sauce
4	46-ounce cans tomato juice

Into a large bowl, mix all ingredients except tomato juice. Blend well. Divide evenly into two 1-gallon containers with tight-fitting lids. Add 2 cans of tomato juice to each container. Cap tightly. Shake once and refrigerate at least 3 days. Strain, reserving liquid. Discard vegetables. Refrigerate. Shake before serving.

Sweet and Sour Salad Dressing

¾	cup sugar
1	small onion, grated
1	teaspoon brown mustard
½	cup red wine vinegar
2	cups vegetable oil

Blend or process ingredients until smooth and light pink. Refrigerate. Shake before using to reblend.

Stuffable Portabello Mushrooms

6   medium (3-5 inch) Portabello mushrooms
1   cup cheap sherry
1   cup red wine vinegar
1-2 cups Italian dressing

Remove stems from mushrooms. Mix all ingredients into a plastic, rubber or glass rectangular bowl. Cover, shake and refrigerate, turning in 6 hours.

Grill or bake, topped with any type of stuffing.

Bay Shrimp Stuffing

This recipe may be used in puff pastry shells, phyllo turnovers or as a topping for mushrooms.

2½ pounds (150-200 count) cooked, peeled tiny shrimp
1   pound soft cream cheese
1   pound provolone cheese, diced
1   medium onion, diced
½   pound button mushrooms, diced
2   roasted bell peppers, diced
1   tablespoon sour cream
1   tablespoon mayonnaise
½   teaspoon each dried basil, tarragon, chives, garlic powder

Squeeze excess moisture from cooked shrimp. Process one pound to paste. Add back with unprocessed shrimp. Add the rest of the ingredients and mix thoroughly. Stuffing should be soft enough to spread. Add sour cream by the teaspoon to thin.

Refrigerate. Stir before using.

Collectors Cafe

7726 N. Kings Highway
Myrtle Beach
(843) 449-9370

Collectors Cafe is a stunning result of business and the arts working hand in hand. It is the only handcrafted restaurant in the area. Owners Michael Smith, Tom Davis and Rhonda Smith are responsible for all of the painting and tile art. Local artists took turns hand-painting bistro tables and the largest original art gallery in the Carolinas is housed under Collectors' roof.

This aesthetic ambience follows through to the kitchen where nary a plate is served without the appearance of an inspired creation. Herbs, sauces and vegetables are not just placed on one's dish, they seem to have been artfully painted there.

Chef Carlos McGrigor broadly strokes the menu with a Mediterranean flair. Not fare for the unadventurous, novel culinary touches are given to all of Collectors' seafood, pastas, beef, veal and lamb. Appetizers of note are a zucchini pancake with lobster and tomato basil cream and a grilled polenta triangle featuring mushroom ragout. Collectors Cafe also offers a European coffee shop, complete with libations from the Godiva Collection.

Although the cafe has only been open for four years, it has certainly made its mark, having been featured in articles in Golf Digest and Southern Living magazines.

Wild and Cultivated Mushroom Soup with Lobster and White Port

1	pound cultivated mushrooms, sliced
¼	pound Shiitake mushrooms, stemmed and sliced
¼	pound Portabello mushrooms, grilled and sliced
1	small carrot, chopped
1	celery rib, chopped
1	small leek, chopped
½	cup dry white wine
¼	cup white port wine
8	ounces heavy cream
16	ounces chicken broth
4	ounces lobster meat, cooked and diced

Fresh tarragon leaves for garnish

Sauté all the vegetables until the cultivated mushrooms give up their liquid. Continue cooking until liquid evaporates and vegetables are lightly browned.

Deglaze the pan with the wine and port. Reduce by one quarter. Then, add in the cream and broth. Reduce heat and simmer for 30 minutes.

Puree the resulting soup with a hand blender. Pour the soup into wide, shallow bowls. Place one ounce of lobster in the center of the bowl and lay 8 to 10 tarragon leaves on top. Serves 4.

Duck Confit with Hummus, Spiced Tomato and Phyllo

For the Duck:

1	leg and 1 thigh from a 4-pound duck

Rendered duck fat

1	bay leaf
4	fresh thyme sprigs
½	teaspoon cracked black peppercorn
½	teaspoon salt

Put all ingredients in a small pot with enough duck fat to cover. Bring to a simmer on the stove. Cover and place in a 350-degree oven for 2½ hours.

Remove and cool. Pick duck meat off, discarding the bones and skin. Reserve at room temperature.

For the Hummus:
10 ounces cooked chick peas
¼ cup Tahini paste
1 lemon, juiced
2 tablespoons roasted garlic
3 tablespoons water

Combine all ingredients into a blender and puree.

For the Spiced Tomato:
1½ pounds tomatoes, seeded, skinned and chopped
½ cup sugar
¼ teaspoon allspice
½ teaspoon cinnamon
¼ teaspoon cloves
½ cup orange juice
¼ cup cornstarch slurry (cornstarch mixed with enough water to create a thin mud)

Simmer the first 6 ingredients in a pot for 15 minutes. Add in the cornstarch to thicken. Cool and set aside at room temperature.

For the Phyllo:
3 phyllo sheets
Extra virgin olive oil

Lay one phyllo sheet on a work surface and brush with olive oil. Lay second phyllo sheet over the first and again, brush with oil. Repeat process with third layer of phyllo.

Cut the sheets into triangles, two inches on all three sides. Bake at 350 degrees until brown.

For Garnish:
Rosemary oil
Fresh rosemary sprigs (if desired)
Baby mizuna leaves
Baby frisee leaves

To Assemble:

Place one heaping tablespoon of hummus in the middle of a plate. Top with one level tablespoon of duck confit, 2 teaspoons of spiced tomato sauce, ½ teaspoon rosemary oil and one triangle of phyllo.

Repeat this process twice more, using all three of the phyllo triangles.

Top with mizuna and frisee leaves. Drizzle tomato sauce and rosemary oil around the plate. If so desired, garnish with sprigs of rosemary. Makes 4 appetizers.

Grilled Salmon Filet with Persian Tabouli and Honey Balsamic Vinaigrette

For the Salmon:
4	7-ounce skinless, boneless salmon filets
1	teaspoon cardamom
1	teaspoon coriander

Mix together the cardamom and coriander. Lightly dust the salmon filets with the spices and grill to medium rare. Set aside.

For the Tabouli:
¼	cup onion
2	garlic cloves, minced
1	tablespoon extra virgin olive oil
1	teaspoon powdered cumin
1	teaspoon powdered cardamom
1	teaspoon powdered ginger
1	teaspoon powdered cinnamon
1	bay leaf
1	pinch saffron threads
¼	cup dried currants
6	whole dried apricots, diced
¼	cup almonds
¼	cup cashews
¼	cup pine nuts
10	ounces chicken broth
10	ounces tabouli
	Butter for sauté

Sauté all of the nuts in butter until brown. Salt to taste and drain. Set aside.

Wilt onion and garlic in the olive oil over medium heat. Then, add in all of the spices, bay leaf, saffron, fruits and nuts. Cook for another 2 minutes.

Deglaze the pan with broth and then pour it over the tabouli in a bowl. Stir and cover for ½ hour.

For the Vinaigrette:
2   tablespoons balsamic vinegar
¼   cup honey
½   cup extra virgin olive oil
Pinch of salt

Pour all ingredients into a blender and puree.

For the Cilantro Oil:
1   cup cilantro leaves, washed
½   cup extra virgin olive oil
Salt to taste

Blanch the cilantro in boiling water for 10 seconds. Place blanched cilantro, olive oil and salt to taste into a blender and puree.

For Garnish:
Roasted red and yellow peppers, diced
Cilantro sprigs

To Assemble:

Mound one cup of tabouli in the center of a plate. Top with a salmon filet. Drizzle cilantro oil and honey vinaigrette around the tabouli and on top of the salmon. Sprinkle the peppers around the tabouli. Top the salmon with sprigs of cilantro. Makes 4 dinners.

Croissants Bakery & Cafe

504-A 27th Avenue North
Myrtle Beach
(843) 448-BAKE

Little did Heidi Schreiner realize when spending childhood summers in Europe with her German grandmother, that she was in training for her adult career as a baker extraordinaire. Now operating the only "corner bakery" and cafe along the Grand Strand, Croissants is a sensual experience for the eyes and nose.

Everything at Croissants is homemade, baked on premise (feast for the nose) and made from scratch every day (feast for the eyes). All of the dessert recipes come from the kitchen of Heidi's mother and grandmother, except for the carrot cake which was perfected by baker Roz Simmons.

Most of Heidi's desserts have a European flair, but her uncommon touch to these usually heavy creations is a lighter genoise cake as the base, which allows diners to enjoy a dessert, even after a four-course meal. The Black Forest and strawberry tortes and chocolate mousse cake give sumptuous credence to this style of baking.

Along with a staggering array of sweets and breads, homemade soups and salads are prepared each day. The chicken salad on a freshly baked croissant is the biggest-selling lunch item. Heidi says her chicken salad is no secret, it's just good quality. Ingredients are cooked all white meat chicken, celery, salt and pepper to taste and "just enough" mayonnaise. Mix all together and enjoy!

Buttercream Icing

This icing is to die for! Use it anytime you can for mouth-watering richness.

1   pound butter
½   pound shortening
3   pounds powdered sugar
1   cup heavy whipping cream
1   teaspoon vanilla

Whip butter until creamy. Add in the shortening and continue whipping until incorporated. Pour in the vanilla. Alternate adding the sugar and cream until all is mixed well and spreadable.

Cream Puffs

½   cup butter
1   cup water
1   cup all-purpose flour, sifted
4   eggs, beaten
Pinch of salt
Peel of ½ lemon, grated
Whipped cream

Melt butter with salt, lemon peel and water in medium saucepan over low heat. When butter has melted, increase heat and bring to a boil. Remove from heat and add all the flour at once. Beat with a wooden spoon until mixture comes away from the sides of the pan.

Return to heat for 1 minute, stirring constantly. Cool slightly, then add eggs a little at a time, beating well between each addition. Put paste in a pastry bag fitted with a fluted nozzle. Pipe rosettes on prepared pan. Bake 20 to 25 minutes at 400 degrees. When cool, fill with whipped cream.

Drunken Jack's
Restaurant & Lounge

4031 U.S. 17 Business
Murrells Inlet
(843) 651-3232

This restaurant pays tribute to the legend of a black-hearted pirate of the 1700s who pillaged the open seas and then buried the highjacked treasures on the tiny islands of Murrells Inlet. After hiding the booty, a celebration lasted for days as Jack and his party feasted on oysters and shrimp from the creeks and washed it down with an inordinate amount of rum – which eventually led to Jack's death.

In business for 18 years now, regular patrons begin their evening on the open-air deck with an appetizer and cocktail. The view is fantastic. The restaurant overlooks the marshes and creeks of Murrells Inlet, where you can spot fishing fleets constantly rolling in to unload fresh catches.

Chef Casey Blake is renowned for loading up plates with generous portions of seafood specialties, marinated chicken, steaks and prime rib. But what customers continually rave about is the accompaniment to every meal – hushpuppies with honey butter. Hushpuppies are a mainstay of Lowcountry cooking and apparently Drunken Jack's has perfected this fried cornmeal delight.

Drunken Jack's popular specialty dinners include a broiled Grouper Royale, topped with lump crabmeat and bernaise sauce; the Robinson Crusoe Special Seafood Coquille, which is a creamy collection of shrimp, scallops and crab; and the Steak Neptune, a delightful plate of grilled filet medallions, shrimp, scallops and lobster, topped with lobster sauce.

Grouper Tasso

To make this dish extra special, top each filet sparingly with hollandaise sauce.

10   6-ounce grouper filets
½   cup clarified butter
Salt and pepper to taste
2   cups flour
10   3-ounce slices of braised ham
2   cups mushrooms, sliced
2   large tomatoes, diced
1   bunch scallions, chopped
¼   cup cilantro, chopped

Heat butter in a large sauté pan and season the grouper filets with salt and pepper.

Dredge the grouper in flour. Place in the hot butter and sauté until cooked to your taste. Set grouper aside. Top each filet with a piece of braised ham and keep warm. Pour off excess butter.

Add mushrooms, tomatoes, scallions and cilantro. Sauté until tender. Pour over the grouper filets and ham. Serve immediately. Makes 10 portions.

Oyster Stew

For true lovers of traditional Lowcountry cuisine, Oyster Stew is just about as down-home as it gets. To be really authentic, be sure to crumble a good amount of crackers into each bowl.

60   select oysters
2   ounces melted butter
½   cup juice from the oysters
½   teaspoon salt
½   teaspoon black pepper
3   cups milk
3   cups half and half cream

Melt butter in a heavy sauce pot. Add oysters, the oyster juice, salt and pepper. Heat until the oysters start to curl and get plump.

Mix in the milk and half and half. Heat until just below the boiling point. Serve immediately. This recipe makes 10 servings.

Sautéed Lump Crab Cakes

Crab cakes can serve as an appetizer or main course. Serve with your favorite sauce, anything from tartar to bernaise.

2	pounds lump crabmeat
1	cup mayonnaise
2	cups breadcrumbs
1	tablespoon parsley, chopped
¼	teaspoon white pepper
½	cup olive oil
4	eggs
2	tablespoons mustard
2	tablespoons Old Bay seasoning

Dash lemon juice

Carefully pick crabmeat free of shells.

When picked clean, combine the crabmeat with all the other ingredients and mix well.

Pat into 3-ounce cakes. Heat the olive oil in a sauté pan and cook crab cakes until golden brown. Makes 10 servings.

Fusco's Restaurant

5308 N. Ocean Boulevard
Beach Colony Resort
Myrtle Beach
(843) 497-0440

An award-winning restaurant, Fusco's is located in one of Myrtle Beach's finest resort hotels and offers a panoramic view of the Atlantic Ocean.

Nick Fusco is the owner and executive chef of this establishment and prides himself in authentic Italian-continental cuisine and for being the only charter member of the American Academy of Chefs currently in Myrtle Beach.

For the most part, Fusco's is set apart from other dining rooms as it is one of the few along the Grand Strand to offer a magnificent champagne Sunday brunch buffet and an Italian food buffet two evenings a week, and a Prime Rib and Pasta buffet on Fridays.

The Fusco brunch offers a wide variety of salads, including crisp favorites, fire and ice and cranberry Waldorf. Warm and comforting items include eggs Benedict, risotto, crepes d'Lorraine, Belgian waffles and quiche. And, of course, bacon, grits and pancakes are a mainstay of the Sunday brunch. For dessert, guests can choose from a table laced with carrot cake, fresh fruit and ambrosia, German chocolate cake and macaroons.

Artichoke Dip

3 14-ounce cans artichoke hearts, drained, finely chopped
1 cup mayonnaise
¼ cup milk
1 cup mozzarella cheese, grated
½ cup Parmesan cheese, grated
2 large garlic cloves, finely chopped

Blend all ingredients together and pour into a casserole dish. Bake at 350 degrees for 30 minutes. Serve with French bread. Serves 6 people as an appetizer.

Eggplant a la Fusco

2 eggplants
1 cup extra virgin olive oil
3 garlic cloves, finely chopped
2 tablespoons fresh Italian parsley, chopped
3 teaspoons salt
¼ teaspoon black pepper

Peel eggplant and slice into ¼-inch thick rounds. Sprinkle with salt and put in a colander for about one hour to allow the water to drain. Blend oil, garlic, ½ teaspoon of salt, pepper and parsley together in a bowl.

Grill drained eggplant slices on both sides until soft and then dip into the oil mixture. Arrange on a serving platter. Serves 6.

Cassata

15 ounces ricotta cheese
¼ cup sugar
3 tablespoons orange liqueur
⅓ cup mixed candied fruit, finely chopped
¼ cup almonds, chopped
1¼ cups semi-sweet mini chocolate chips, divided
1 prepared pound cake (10¾ ounces)
1 teaspoon instant coffee, dissolved in ¼ cup boiling water
6 tablespoons unsalted butter or margarine, cut into 8 pieces and chilled

With an electric mixer, combine ricotta cheese, sugar and liqueur. Beat until light and fluffy, about 3 minutes. Fold in candied fruit, chopped almonds and ¼ cup of the chocolate chips. Set aside.

Cut the pound cake, horizontally, in four layers. Place top layer of cake, cut side down, on a serving platter. Spread one-third of the cheese mixture evenly over cake layer. Repeat this procedure twice more and then top with the last cake layer. Press lightly to compact cake and cheese filling. Cover with plastic wrap and chill for at least 2 hours.

Meanwhile, put remaining 1 cup of chocolate chips and coffee in the top of a double boiler over hot, but not boiling, water. Stir constantly until the chocolate is melted. Add butter pieces, one at a time, stirring constantly, until all the butter is added and incorporated. Remove from heat and chill to spreading consistency, about 2 to 2½ hours.

Spread the top and sides of the cake with the chilled frosting. If you like, sprinkle the top with chopped almonds. Serves 12.

Tip: This cake can be made one day in advance, covered with plastic wrap and refrigerated. Let stand at room temperature for about 30 minutes before slicing.

Aragosta Fra Diavolo Romeo

(Lobster in Red Sauce)

12	littleneck clams
2	live lobsters (1½ pounds each)
¼	cup olive oil
2	whole garlic cloves
¼	cup cognac
2	pounds tomatoes, peeled and chopped
1½	teaspoons salt
⅛	teaspoon crushed, dried red pepper
½	teaspoon oregano

Chopped parsley for garnish

Scrub the clams and wash under cold running water. Wash the lobsters, chop off the claws and crack them. Split the bodies in half, remove the black vein and sack, then cut each body portion in half again, crosswise. (Have the fish market do this for you, if you prefer). Heat the oil in a casserole dish or deep skillet. Place the garlic and lobsters in it, flesh side down. Cook until the garlic browns, then discard the cloves. Add the cognac, cover and cook for 2 minutes. Add in the tomatoes, salt, red pepper and oregano. Cook over medium heat for 15 minutes. Add the clams, cover and cook for 10 minutes longer.

Sprinkle with chopped parsley to garnish and serve with sautéed Italian bread. Serves 4.

GIOVANNI'S

**A TOUCH
OF ITALY**

Giovanni's

504 27th Avenue North
Myrtle Beach
(843) 626-8995

Giovanni's is one of those places of character, the tone set by the indomitable personality of owner and chef Giovanni Carandola. He regularly wanders through the dining room asking patrons how their meal is in a voice that seems to come from the dredging depths of a gravel pit. Framed photographs of himself with recognizable celebrities beam down from the walls and he takes equal pride in the preparation and presentation of every dish served. Giovanni's is, without a doubt, Giovanni Carandola.

The menu is a vast array of Northern and Central Italian gourmet cuisine. Carandola makes a point of improving a recipe and constantly shops for unique ingredients that will punctuate the taste of a particular dish. As Giovanni says, "If only you had to follow a recipe, then anyone could be a chef."

Intimate in atmosphere, Giovanni's is a beautifully appointed restaurant and lounge done in deep greens, rich woods and boasting a yawning fireplace that's in full flame on chilly nights.

Ossobuco Alla Milanese

(Braised Veal Shank)

This method of preparing Ossobuco is typical of Lombardi, and more precisely, of Milan.

4   1½-inch thick veal shanks, cut from the middle of the shin
4   tablespoons olive oil
1   pound canned, Italian-style peeled tomatoes, strained of half the juice
1   cup dry red wine
1   small onion, diced
All-purpose flour for dusting
Salt and freshly ground black pepper to taste
1   large orange

Juice the orange and set liquid aside. Grate the rind of half the orange and also set aside.

Dust the veal shanks with salt and flour. Heat the olive oil in a cast iron casserole and sauté the shanks two at a time on both sides, taking great care not to damage the marrow in the center or let the marrow fall out.

Remove the shanks from the casserole and set aside. In the same oil, sauté the onion until transparent. Then add the tomatoes, breaking them up with a wooden spoon. Cook over high heat so the tomatoes can reduce.

After 5 minutes, add in the orange juice, orange rind and red wine. Return the shanks to the sauce, still over high heat.

Season to taste with salt and pepper and then reduce the heat. Cover the casserole and simmer for one to 1½ hours or until the meat begins to come away from the bone. Serves 4.

Minestrone Alla Milanese

2   ounces prosciutto, cut into strips
2   ounces butter
2   garlic cloves, coarsely chopped
3   tablespoons Italian parsley, coarsely chopped
2   zucchinis, cubed
2   carrots, cubed

2 celery stalks, cubed
2 ripe tomatoes, finely chopped
2 potatoes, cubed
6 ounces fresh borlotti beans or 1 medium can
12 ounces Savoy cabbage, cut into strips
1 fresh rosemary sprig
10 ounces pork rind, without the fat
8 cups broth or stock
1 cup arborio rice
¾ cup freshly grated Parmesan cheese
Several sage leaves
Nutmeg
Salt and freshly ground black pepper

Place the prosciutto strips in a large, heavy saucepan with the butter and sauté over moderate heat for 5 minutes. Add in the garlic and sauté for another 2 minutes.

Then add the parsley, zucchini, carrots, celery, tomatoes, potatoes, fresh borlotti beans (if you're using canned beans, add them later), cabbage, rosemary and sage.

Sprinkle the pork rind generously with nutmeg, salt and pepper. Roll and bind the seasoned pork rind with kitchen string. Add the prepared pork to the saucepan, along with enough broth to thoroughly cover the vegetables. Bring to a boil and then simmer for at least one hour.

Add in more broth if necessary. Season to taste with salt and pepper and stir in the rice (if you are using canned borlotti beans, add them at this point). Cook for another 20 minutes or so, stirring frequently and mashing some of the potato cubes to give the soup a thicker consistency. Serve with a slice of the pork rind roll in each bowl and sprinkle with Parmesan cheese. Serves 6 to 8.

Linguine Alla Giovanni

4 pounds mussels
2 pounds Cherry Stone clams
1¼ pounds shrimp
1¼ pounds sea scallops
6 tablespoons extra virgin olive oil
2 pounds Italian-style peeled tomatoes

47

1½ cups yellow onions, chopped
2   garlic cloves, chopped
1   pound linguine
1   tablespoon Italian parsley, chopped
Salt and freshly ground black pepper to taste

Scrub the mussels and clams under cool water. Place the mussels, clams, shrimp and scallops in a heavy skillet. Add in 3 tablespoons of the olive oil and the garlic cloves. Cover and place over moderate heat until the mussel and clam shells open (about 5 to 7 minutes).

In a wide skillet over low heat, warm 3 tablespoons of olive oil, add the onion and peeled tomatoes. Fry gently, stirring frequently, until the onion is translucent (about 6 minutes).

Then add all of the seafood to the onion and tomatoes and cook for 3 minutes. Meanwhile, cook linguine until al dente. Transfer the pasta to a warm serving dish and pour the sauce over it. Sprinkle the parsley over the whole plate. Serves 6.

Saltimbocca Alla Romana

(Veal scallops with prosciutto, sage and mushrooms)
12   2- to 3-ounce veal scallops (escalopes)
1   teaspoon ground dried sage
6   slices prosciutto, halved
2½ ounces butter
½   cup dry white wine
¼   pound fresh mushrooms, sliced
Salt to taste

Flatten each veal scallop with a meat mallet. Dust them on both sides with the ground sage. On each slice of veal, place a piece of the prosciutto and secure with a toothpick.

Heat butter in a large, heavy skillet and brown the scallops over moderate to high heat for 3 minutes. Turn gently and cook for 2 minutes. Sprinkle the fresh mushrooms and wine over the scallops and cook for another 3 minutes.

Arrange the veal on a serving dish, prosciutto side up. Stir 2 tablespoons of water into the pan juices and let boil for 1 minute. Check seasoning and adjust to taste. Spoon the pan sauce over the meat and serve at once. Serves 6.

Salmon Alla Salvia

(Baby Coco Salmon with Sage)
4   7- to 8-ounce salmon steaks
All-purpose flour for dusting
3   ounces butter
4   bay leaves
8-10 sage leaves or 1½ teaspoons of dried sage
¼   cup brandy

Wash the salmon and pat dry. Lightly dust with the flour.

Place butter, bay leaves and sage in a skillet over high heat. Sauté until the butter is a golden brown. Then place the salmon in the hot skillet and fry over high heat, turning only once, until the skins are crunchy and golden (about 5 minutes).

Add in the brandy, cooking for another 5 minutes over moderate heat. Serve immediately on warmed plates and garnish with the cooked sage and bay leaves. Makes 4 servings.

Costolette In Agrodolce

(Veal Chops in Sweet and Sour Sauce)
6   veal chops, lightly pounded
2   tablespoons raisins
1   egg, slightly beaten
1¾ cups dry breadcrumbs
2   tablespoons sugar
1   tablespoon potato flour (or cornstarch)
1   cup vinegar, red wine and water mixed in equal parts
Salt and pepper to taste

Soak raisins in warm water for 30 minutes and drain.

Dip each chop on both sides in the beaten eggs and then coat with breadcrumbs.

Heat the butter in a heavy frying pan, large enough to hold the veal chops in one layer. Cook each chop on both sides over moderate heat until a golden color. Drain on paper towels and keep warm. Pour off the fat from the pan.

Dissolve the sugar in the pan over moderate heat and mix in the potato flour or cornstarch. When it begins to show color, stir in the vinegar and wine mixture, stirring continuously until slightly thickened.

Replace the veal chops in the pan, side by side, and sprinkle in the raisins and salt and pepper to taste. Cover and cook for another 5 minutes over low heat.

Arrange the chops on a platter, cover with the sauce and serve while hot. Serves 6.

Cozze Ripiene
(Stuffed Mussels or Clams in a Half Shell)

In Livorno, the stuffed mussels or clams differ from those of other regions, due to the addition of a little sausage meat to the classic mixture of herbs and breadcrumbs.

7	ounces sweet Italian sausage, skinned and crumbled
3	tablespoons fine dry breadcrumbs
2	tablespoons flat-leaf, Italian parsley, chopped
2	garlic cloves, chopped
2	plum tomatoes, peeled and chopped
1	egg
5	pounds large mussels or clams
2	tablespoons extra virgin olive oil

Salt to taste

In a mixing bowl, combine the sausage, 2 tablespoons of the breadcrumbs, the parsley, garlic, tomatoes and egg. Season with salt to taste. Mix well and set aside.

Scrub and debeard (if using mussels) the shellfish. Place shellfish in a shallow saucepan, cover and put over moderate heat until the shells open in about 5 to 7 minutes. Remove from the heat and discard any mussels or clams that did not open. Open each shell, discarding the top shell.

With a small, sharp knife, loosen the meat from the bottom of the shells and leave them nestled there.

Preheat the oven to 350 degrees. Divide the sausage mixture among the shells, mounding it on top. Sprinkle each with the remaining 1 tablespoon of breadcrumbs and the olive oil.

Arrange the shells on a flat, ovenproof pan and bake for 15 minutes. Serve very hot. Makes 6 portions as an appetizer.

Cannoli Alla Siciliana

For the Cannoli:

2   cups all-purpose flour
1   cup granulated sugar
1   tablespoon cocoa powder
1   tablespoon ground cinnamon
4   tablespoons butter
¼   cup Marsala wine
1   egg, beaten
12   cannoli tubes (special metal pastry cylinders)
7½   cups oil for deep frying

For the Filling:

2¼   cups ricotta cheese
¼   cup candied orange peel, diced
¼   cup candicd citron pccl, diced
¼   cup candied cherries
½   cup confectioners' icing sugar
⅓   cup bitter chocolate, coarsely grated

Make a dough by mixing together the flour, a ¼ cup of the granulated sugar, cocoa powder, a pinch of cinnamon, the butter and Marsala wine. Knead until smooth and roll into a thin sheet. Cut the dough into 4- to 5-inch rounds and wrap each one around a cannoli tube. Seal the sides where they join by brushing with the beaten egg. Deep fry the cannoli tubes in very hot oil. Drain on paper towels. When cool, carefully slide each out of the metal cylinders.

Rub the ricotta cheese with the rest of the cinnamon and granulated sugar through a sieve. Add the candied orange and citron peels, blending thoroughly. Fill the cannoli using a piping pastry bag. Decorate each with a cherry at each end. Dust with the icing sugar and chocolate. Makes 12 desserts.

Hard Rock Cafe

1322 Celebrity Circle
Broadway At The Beach
Myrtle Beach
(843) 946-0007

Emulating an Egyptian pyramid, this Hard Rock Cafe is the 42nd addition to the company's international roster. Like all of its cousins, this location celebrates the history of rock 'n' roll music and culture with authentic memorabilia throughout the restaurant.

Formidable sphinxes lie in wait at the entrance, lit by gas torches. The structure is surrounded by waterfalls, palm trees and columns relating the mysteries of hieroglyphics. And, of course, inside and out, rock 'n' roll music beats in time with your heart.

The ambience may have you conjuring up visions of gliding across the River Nile, but the food will promptly land you right back in America's Heartland.

The pulse of the kitchen is found at a huge smoker-rotisserie which, at any given time, is slowly and deliberately preparing up to 350 pounds of pork. No meat is served until it has spent 12 hours in the smoker. When it's done, the pork will be hand-shredded. This process is time intensive, but it is the only method that assures the meat is of the utmost tenderness, infused completely with a smoky flavor and free of excess fat.

As you would surmise, Hard Rock's most-ordered dish is the BBQ Pig Sandwich served with crunchy cole slaw tingling with a vinegar and sugar dressing and pinto beans tossed with the delectable slow-roasted meat and signature barbecue sauce.

Buffalo Chicken Sandwich

This recipe is a tangy alternative to the basic battered and fried chicken sandwich. Add to the zest by using a spicier wing sauce and cool it down to your own preference with bleu cheese.

10   boneless chicken breasts
10   hamburger buns
10   tomato slices
6   eggs
1   quart flour
1   quart milk
2   quarts Buffalo wing sauce
1   head of shredded lettuce
Creamy bleu cheese dressing

On a flat surface, lay chicken breasts out and pound lightly. Place flour in a cake pan. In another bowl, mix eggs and milk together. Place chicken pieces in the flour and cover completely. Then place the floured breasts in the egg and milk wash, cover thoroughly, and then dredge the chicken in the flour once more. Cook the prepared chicken in a fryer at 325 degrees for 6 to 8 minutes or until done.

Toast the top cover of each bun. On the bottom half of the bun, place the cooked chicken breast and pour wing sauce over it. Top the wing sauce with the bleu cheese dressing, or if you prefer, serve the cheese on the side. Finish off the sandwich with shredded lettuce and a slice of tomato. Makes 10 servings.

Chinese Chicken Salad

This Eastern version of a chicken salad creates a taste sensation with its use of crunchy vegetables, a light peanut base and the smack of lime.

10   boneless chicken breasts
10   snow peas
2   quarts peanut base Oriental sauce
3   heads of iceberg lettuce
1   carrot, peeled
4   ounces water chestnuts
1   bunch of fresh broccoli
Lime juice

HARD ROCK RECIPES CONTINUED

Cilantro
Mandarin oranges and sliced red peppers for garnish

Place chicken on a flat surface and pound lightly. Using the Oriental sauce as a marinade, pour enough to cover the chicken in a bowl. Cover and refrigerate for 2 hours. Cook the chicken in the oven or on a BBQ grill until done.

Slice carrots, broccoli and cut snow peas in half. Bring a pot of water to a boil on the stove and cook the vegetables al dente: slightly cooked, but still firm. Drain the vegetables. Slice the chicken into one-inch strips lengthwise and then cut again crosswise into bite-sized pieces. In a large mixing bowl, chop the lettuce, add the water chestnuts and cooked vegetables. Mix in chicken pieces.

Create the dressing by pouring Oriental sauce into a bowl and carefully adding lime juice and cilantro to taste. Pour dressing over the salad mixture and toss together. Garnish with sweet mandarin orange sections and sliced red bell peppers if desired. Makes 10 salads.

Caribbean Jerk Sandwich

When it comes to spicing, Jerks are starting to take over from Cajuns. Proper "jerking" slides sweetly past your tongue, only to surprise your throat with a burst of heat. Hard Rock chef Victor Colbert creates his own jerk seasoning by experimentation. You, too, can be your own culinary chemist. Head to your spice cabinet and pull out the cinnamon, allspice, nutmeg, cayenne pepper, rosemary and salt. Mix all of these aromatic and distinct spices together until you find your own perfect jerk.

10   boneless chicken breasts
10   hamburger buns
10   tomato slices
2   cups salad oil
1   head of lettuce
1   tablespoon mayonnaise
¼   cup jerk seasoning (Mix your own or buy at a grocery store)
10   slices Monterey Jack cheese

In a quart bowl, place seasoning and salad oil and blend together. Lay out chicken breasts on a flat surface and pound lightly. Place pounded chicken pieces in the seasoning and oil and marinate, covered in the refrigerator, for 2 hours. Cook the chicken in the oven or on a BBQ grill until done. In the last minutes of cooking, place a slice of cheese overtop each chicken breast until melted.

Place each piece of chicken and cheese on a toasted bun and cover with lettuce and tomato. Spread mayonnaise on the top half of the bun or serve on the side.

House of Blues

4640 U.S. 17 South
Barefoot Landing
North Myrtle Beach
(843) 272-3000

Built to resemble a "juke joint" of the deep South, the House of Blues is a music hall, restaurant and museum of "Outsider" art. Similar to the musical genre known as the blues, the artwork displayed here shows emotion rather than schooling; indicative of personality quirks, rather than impressions on canvas.

Needless to say, House of Blues sticks primarily to Southern-inspired cooking with menu selections such as jambalaya, etouffee and bread pudding. It also hosts a Sunday gospel brunch, serving up a full buffet of breakfast and lunch items while presenting some of the best gospel artists and choirs in the area.

Whether visiting the House of Blues for food or music, this venue is certainly a cultural destination that embraces all families of entertainment and spotlights the artistic evolution of Southern culture.

House of Blues Catfish Bites

5	pounds catfish
½	gallon oil
4½	cups milk
2	tablespoons cayenne pepper
3	tablespoons salt
1½	tablespoons black pepper
4	cups flour
2	cups corn flour

Cut the catfish into bite-sized pieces.

Make a wet batter by combining the milk, one tablespoon of cayenne pepper, 1 tablespoon of salt, ½ tablespoon black pepper and 3 cups of flour. Mix well and set aside.

Create a dry coating by mixing together the corn flour, 1 tablespoon of cayenne pepper, 2 tablespoons of salt, 1 tablespoon of black pepper and 1 cup of flour.

Soak the catfish pieces in the wet batter and then coat generously in the dry mixture. Fry the prepared catfish bites in the oil at 350 degrees for 3 to 4 minutes. Serve with tartar sauce and a lemon wedge if you so desire.

House of Blues Rosemary Chicken Marinade

2½	quarts vegetable oil
⅓	quart lemon juice
⅓	quart lime juice
⅓	cup rosemary
⅓	cup garlic
½	cup fresh orange juice
¼	cup Worcestershire sauce
¼	cup Tabasco sauce
¼	cup coarse black pepper
¼	cup salt
1	Spanish onion, diced
⅓	cup honey

Combine all ingredients together. Marinate your chicken in the mixture in the refrigerator for at least 24 hours.

The
Library

European and Continental Cuisine

A Restaurant of Excellence

The Library

1212 N. Kings Highway
Myrtle Beach
(843) 448-4527

Breaking out the bow tie and tails would be perfectly appropriate attire for dining at The Library. This candlelight and white linen establishment is an exceptional dining pleasure and a first-hand lesson in superb service.

As if by mental telepathy, your every need and want is anticipated and met at The Library by an expert, tuxedo-clad staff. It is no wonder that this 24-year-old restaurant consistently receives local and national recognition. Seventy percent of The Library's business is composed of repeat customers and word-of-mouth recommendation.

High recommendation of The Library also comes from Mobil Travel Guide, which consistently has given this upscale venue its 3-Star rating since 1980. With only 2,700 similarly rated restaurants in the United States, it is a coveted distinction and the only such recipient on the Grand Strand.

From the unusual to the sublime, the menu offers a French continental fare, spiced by such rare treats as sweetbreads and steak tartare. The Library's staff is not only painstakingly trained in service, but often prepares tableside meals. The intimate dining room is forever sizzling as waitstaff creates steak Diane, rack of lamb, steak au poivre, Chateaubriand, Caesar salad and flaming desserts, right before your eyes.

Chicken and Shrimp

1   8-ounce chicken breast, deboned and slightly pounded
2   16/20-count size shrimp, cooked and cooled
Butter for sautéing
Flour for dusting
1   clove garlic, minced
½   teaspoon hacomat (a seasoning available in specialty stores)
1   teaspoon dry demi-glace
2   stalks white asparagus, cooked al dente
¼   cup hollandaise sauce
Fresh chopped parsley for garnish

Place a sauté pan on high and when it is hot, add enough butter to cover the bottom. Stir in the garlic, hacomat and dry demi-glace. Lightly flour the chicken and carefully place it in the pan. Brown evenly on one side. Then, flip it over and cook until done.

Arrange chicken on an entree plate. Split each asparagus spear lengthwise, but do not cut completely in half. Arrange the asparagus, end to end, on top of the chicken breast and cover only the spear with hollandaise sauce. Place under a broiler until the hollandaise is braised. Place the 2 shrimp on top of the meat arranged behind the asparagus. Garnish with chopped parsley and serve at once. Makes 1 dinner.

Potato Onion Roquefort Soup

4   large potatoes
2   large onions
1½ gallons + 1 pint chicken broth
1   pint white wine
2   ounces half and half cream per bowl served
½   ounce Roquefort cheese crumbles per bowl served
Salt and pepper to taste

Peel and cut up onions julienne style. Peel and cut potatoes to a medium-size dice. Place stock in a sauce pot, add onions and potatoes and bring to a boil. Cover pot and let simmer on lower heat for one hour.

Run the cooked soup through a food processor until very smooth. Season to taste with salt and pepper. Top each bowl of soup with 2 ounces of half and half cream and ½ ounce of Roquefort cheese crumbles.

Littles At The Beach Restaurant

411 79th Avenue North
Myrtle Beach
(843) 449-3678

Although prime rib accounts for more than one-third of food sales at Littles, owner Frank Dowling has brought unique culinary experiences and tastes to his Myrtle Beach restaurant, culled from a lifetime of extensive travel.

As pertains to the Grand Strand, Littles will be the only dining establishment where one can find the delightfully sweet delicacy, lobster dainties. A pygmy breed of the shellfish, "dainties" hail exclusively from two opposite ends of the world – Iceland or South America. Here, too, is the home of the only Irish Tea served in town; a combination of an Irish tea blend, amaretto liqueur and whipped cream.

A play on the usual recipe for Oysters Rockefeller has become a signature dish at Littles. The expected became the sublime by adding a touch of Ouzo – a Greek, aniseed-flavored spirit – and crowning the oysters with a homemade red garlic sauce.

Dowling insists that his recipes are not as complicated as diners think: The trick is in the cooking. Chef William Harley has commandeered Littles' kitchen since it opened 15 years ago and Dowling claims that Harley has a "touch" when preparing food that is unparalleled and knows how to expertly use paprika, a spice most often ignored in this region. What new surprises may be in store for regular patrons of Littles? It is fast becoming one of the best-known "chop houses" in the area, offering pork, lamb and veal.

Chicken Saltimbocca

Garlic sauce (recipe follows)
Spinach topping (recipe follows)
2   boneless, skinless chicken breasts
2   tablespoons butter or margarine
Flour
2   thin slices of Swiss cheese

Garlic Sauce

½   cup tomato sauce
Scant ¼ teaspoon each of basil and oregano
2   tablespoons water
2   tablespoons olive oil
Salt and pepper to taste
¼   teaspoon garlic, finely chopped

Mix together all ingredients and set aside.

Spinach Topping

1   teaspoon onion, chopped
1   tablespoon butter or margarine
1   slice bacon, cooked crisp and crumbled
1   teaspoon anisette (optional)
¼   cup prepared garlic sauce
½   cup frozen chopped spinach, pressed dry

In a microwave oven or skillet, cook the chopped onion and butter or margarine until clear, but not brown.

Add in the crumbled bacon, anisette if you wish and ¼ cup of the prepared garlic sauce. Stir together and remove from heat.

Fold in the spinach. Set aside.

Preparing the Dish

Heat 2 tablespoons of butter or margarine in a skillet over medium heat. Dredge the chicken breasts in flour. Cook the chicken until browned and then lower the heat and cook for another 5 minutes.

Top each chicken breast with 1 tablespoon of the spinach mixture and a slice of Swiss cheese. Top all of this with the remaining ¼ cup of garlic sauce. Sauté for another 2 to 3 minutes.

Transfer each chicken breast to an oven-proof plate and broil until the top is a golden brown. Serves 2.

Strawberries O'Neil

½	cup fresh strawberries, sliced
⅓	cup sour cream
½	cup brown sugar
	Amaretto to drizzle

Mix together the sour cream and brown sugar. Place half of the cream sauce into a stemmed parfait or sherbet glass.

Top with the sliced strawberries and drizzle with amaretto. Add the rest of the cream sauce over the strawberries. Top with a whole fresh strawberry for garnish.

Makes 1 dessert.

Littles Cole Slaw

1	onion, finely chopped
1	head of cabbage, sliced
1	cup white vinegar
⅓	cup water
1	cup sugar
1⅓	teaspoons salt
1	teaspoon celery seed
⅓	cup oil

In a saucepan combine vinegar, water, sugar, salt and celery seed. Bring to a boil. Add in the oil. Bring to a boil a second time.

Pour over cabbage and onions. Stir and refrigerate.

MYRTLE BEACH, SC

Magoo's Fine Food, Sports & Spirits

905 Oak Street
Myrtle Beach
(843) 946-6683

A thoroughly locals pub and restaurant, Magoo's is located in what used to be the first ice house in Myrtle Beach which later became a popular fish market. Over the three years of its operation, Magoo's has evolved into a dart emporium with an extensive imported and microbrew beer selection and an area hangout that offers a broad food menu.

With the exception of a few appetizers, all of Magoo's dishes are homemade, to order. The chicken wings have to be the house bestsellers that come in three delicious flavors, well worth every napkin required. Traditional Buffalo-style wings can be ordered mild, regular or as hot as you can stand. Parmesan-garlic wings are dripping in butter and cheese, the teriyaki version seems to be the perfect marriage of sweet and sour. A regular customer launched the now popular Jo-Jo wings, which are fried extra-crispy and generously coated with salt and pepper.

Other Magoo darlings are a variety of quesadillas and the prime rib and marinated ribeye steak dinners served with garlic mashed potatoes. These cuts of prepared meat take up nearly the whole plate for a price that doesn't come close to emptying your wallet.

Magoo's Marinated Ribeye Steak

3-4 ribeye steaks
½ cup soy sauce
½ cup Worcestershire sauce
½ cup red Cabernet wine
1 tablespoon Cajun spice
1 tablespoon granulated garlic

Mix all ingredients together in a container large enough to hold the steaks. Marinate the meat for 2 to 4 hours and then grill to desired doneness. For a spicier taste, add extra Cajun seasoning to the marinade or coat each steak with the spice while cooking. This marinade also works well with flank steak if you marinate it overnight.

Beer Battered Chicken Fingers

1½ cups flour for batter
¾ cup flour for coating
1½ cups beer
1½ tablespoons Lawry's Season Salt
½ teaspoon paprika
¼ tablespoon black pepper
¼ tablespoon granulated garlic
2-3 pounds of fresh chicken breasts
Honey mustard and/or ranch dressing for dipping

Mix together 1½ cups of flour and all other dry ingredients thoroughly. Add in beer and mix until all lumps disappear and the consistency is that of thick pancake batter.

Cut chicken breasts into ¼-inch strips. Dip the strips into the batter and coat well. Dredge the coating strips in the remaining ¾ cup of flour. Fry until golden brown. Note: Only prepare enough strips at one time to have enough cooking room in the fryer or the fingers will not come out crispy.

Magoo's Parmesan Wings

4-5 pounds chicken wings
1 cup butter
½ cup olive oil
1 tablespoon granulated garlic powder
¾ cup Parmesan cheese, grated
Parsley flakes

Grill, bake or fry chicken wings to desired doneness.

In a microwaveable container, mix together the butter, oil and garlic powder. Cover with plastic wrap and microwave just until the butter is thoroughly melted. Take out of the oven and stir in the Parmesan cheese.

Pour the coating mix into a large, deep container with a lid. Add in the hot, cooked chicken wings and shake to coat well. Lay out the coated wings on a serving tray and sprinkle with more grated Parmesan cheese and parsley flakes.

Serve with bleu cheese or ranch dressing.

The Mayor's House Restaurant

2614 U.S. 17 South
Litchfield Beach
(843) 237-9082

The Mayor's House has always been synonymous with elite dining and clientele, unique decor and a romantic mood. Owners Chet and Karen Herman actively participate in creating their restaurant's fine ambience by performing on weekends, playing the saxophone and guitar and singing for their dining guests. Gourmet chefs grace the kitchens of this restaurant, offering American, French and continental cuisine.

No matter how time-consuming or difficult, chef Ken Stinson and his crew insist on doing things "the old-fashioned way." Everything is made from scratch to order with soups and sauces prepared each day. Diners return again and again to The Mayor's House to experience one of the chef's special dishes.

The Mayor's House receives rave reviews from patrons when Shrimp Dominique is featured – jumbo shrimp stuffed with Dijon mustard and cheddar cheese, wrapped in sizzling bacon and topped with Bearnaise sauce. Other culinary delights originating from this kitchen are lobster and seafood bog, bouillabaisse and creme brulee.

Sesame and Poppy Seed Encrusted Grouper with Sesame Soy Sauce

1   6-8 ounce grouper filet
2   tablespoons sesame seeds
1   tablespoon poppy seeds
2   cups all-purpose flour
1   teaspoon Old Bay Seasoning
2   cups milk
2   eggs
Olive oil for cooking
Sesame Soy Sauce (recipe follows)

Mix flour and Old Bay Seasoning together in a small bowl and set aside. Beat the milk and eggs together in another small bowl to make an egg wash and set aside.

Place the filet in the flour mixture and then in the egg wash. Drain most of the liquid off of the fish. Repeat this process until a paste-like coating forms on the grouper.

Sprinkle half of the sesame and poppy seeds on a flat surface or plate. Press the fish into the seed mixture. Turn over, and coat the other side of the grouper with the rest of the seeds.

Place enough oil in a sauté pan to cover the bottom and place over medium high heat. When hot, put coated fish in the pan and cook for 3 minutes or until lightly browned. Turn and brown fish on the other side, cooking for about 5 minutes. Pour a small amount of the Sesame Soy Sauce on a plate. Place the fish on top and then pour the rest of the sauce over to serve. Makes 1 portion.

Sesame Soy Sauce

1   ounce sesame oil
2   ounces Yoshida's Gourmet Sauce
2   ounces white wine
3   ounces honey

Over medium heat in a saucepan, place the sesame oil, Yoshida's Gourmet Sauce, white wine and honey. Stir occasionally until the mixture comes to a boil.

Black Bean Cakes with Sour Cream Sauce

3	cups dried black beans
12	cups water
6	chicken bouillon cubes
1	small yellow onion, minced
1	teaspoon garlic powder
1	small red pepper, minced
1	teaspoon cumin
2	tablespoons dried cilantro
1	teaspoon blackening seasoning
2	cups breadcrumbs
½	cup flour

Olive oil for cooking
Sour Cream Sauce (recipe follows)

Place black beans, chicken bouillon cubes and water in a heavy saucepan and bring them to a boil. Then, reduce heat and cook for about 2 hours or until the beans are softened.

Combine the onion, red pepper and spices with the cooked black beans and cook for another 30 minutes or until most of the liquid is absorbed and the consistency is thick.

Transfer to a large mixing bowl and add in the flour and breadcrumbs. Mix well until you have achieved a creamy texture. Let this mixture cool and then form into cakes.

Pour a small amount of oil in a sauté pan and place over medium heat. Cook the bean cakes for 3 to 4 minutes on each side. Serve with the sour cream sauce

Sour Cream Sauce

1	cup sour cream
½	cup heavy cream
2	ounces white wine

Place all ingredients in a saucepan over high heat. Reduce to half the original volume. Serve this sauce warm over Black Bean Cakes.

Milky Way Cheesecake (pictured on the cover)

- 1½ cups chocolate graham cracker crumbs
- 1 cup toasted almond crumbs
- 1⅓ cups sugar
- 6 tablespoons butter
- 24 ounces cream cheese, softened
- 4 eggs
- ⅔ cup heavy whipping cream
- ⅓ cup Creme de Cacao syrup
- 1 teaspoon vanilla
- 6 ounces caramel sauce
- 12 ounces semi-sweet chocolate

Blend graham cracker crumbs, ⅓ cup sugar and toasted almond crumbs together. Add in the butter and mix until the ingredients all hold together. Grease a 10-inch springform pan with butter. Press the mixture to the edges and cover the bottom of the pan until a firm crust is formed.

Mix the softened cream cheese and 1 cup of sugar together until creamy. Beat in the eggs, one at a time, until the mixture is smooth. Add the Creme de Cacao, vanilla and ⅓ cup whipping cream and beat until light. Pour this into the crust and bake in a 350-degree oven for 55 minutes or until the cake rises evenly and starts to crack around the edges.

Remove cake from the oven and let cool for one hour at room temperature. When cooled, pour the caramel over the top and spread evenly. Place the cake in the refrigerator, lightly covered, overnight.

Put the semi-sweet chocolate and ⅓ cup whipping cream in a double boiler and blend until all of the chocolate is melted and the mixture is smooth. Cut the cake into slices and place them on a pan or serving plate. Spoon the chocolate glaze over each slice. Place the cake in the refrigerator for one hour or until the chocolate sets.

The Melting Pot

5001 N. Kings Highway
Myrtle Beach
(843) 692-9003

The Melting Pot offers the Grand Strand its only fondue restaurant. Opened in July 1996, The Melting Pot is truly a unique dining experience. Perhaps because you're cooking your own dinner, mouthful by mouthful, supping at The Melting Pot tends to be conducive to lively conversation and a longer-than-usual, relaxing stay.

Each table is equipped with its own central hotplate, regulated by the wait staff, to keep your pot of bubbling cooking oil, low-fat broth, cheese or chocolate at just the right temperature. Chunks of food for dipping are amazingly fresh and cut to just the right size to stay on your fondue fork, from pot to mouth. Vegetables are neon-bright in color and crunchy fresh; fruits are cut immediately prior to serving to maintain texture and deter browning.

Originating in Maitland, Fla., in 1975, there are now nearly 50 Melting Pots across the nation. Myrtle Beach's Melting Pot is owned by Keith Dunn and Buddy Cribb, two native sons who continue this franchise's long-standing tradition of "hands-on" proprietors. In its first year of operation, this restaurant won the chainwide service award.

Kirschwasser Swiss Cheese Fondue

8	ounces dry white wine
2	cups Gruyere Swiss Cheese, shredded
2	cups Emmenthaler Swiss Cheese, shredded
⅓	cup all-purpose flour
1	lemon
1	teaspoon minced garlic
1	ounce Kirschwasser Cherry Brandy

Nutmeg and black peppercorn to taste

Dipping Foods:

• French, rye and pumpernickel breads, cut into 1-inch cubes

• Golden delicious apples, sliced into bite-sized cubes (squeeze ½ of the lemon into a container of ice water and put sliced apples into it to prevent browning).

• Cleaned and cut fresh vegetables such as celery, carrots, cauliflower and so on.

Fill a fondue pot or the bottom of a double boiler with approximately one inch of water and turn the burner on low. Your top liner should be large enough to hold all of the ingredients. Pour the white wine into liner.

Combine the two shredded cheeses in a tightly lidded container. Add in the flour, seal and shake vigorously, being sure to coat all of the cheese. Set aside.

Turn the burner to high and wait about 5 minutes or until steam appears. Add in the garlic and squeeze one-half of the lemon into the wine base. Using tongs, slowly add cheese mixture to wine base, starting with about 3 tongs, and begin mixing. Continue adding small amounts of cheese until you achieve the consistency of warm honey.

Add about 3 shakes of nutmeg and 5 turns of fresh cracked peppercorn. Blend together. Add in the cherry brandy and fold until completely blended. Remove from burner altogether or turn to low. Now you're ready to grab the fondue fork, attach foods and dip.

*Caution: As cheese gets lower in the liner as you eat, the temperature will become hotter.

Cookies & Cream Marshmallow Dream Chocolate Fondue

1   pound sweet gourmet Swiss chocolate
⅓   cup whole milk
1   tablespoon marshmallow cream
3   Oreo cookies, crushed
1   ounce Bacardi 151 Rum
Dipping Foods:
Marshmallows cut in half and rolled in chopped nuts, strawberries, pineapple, cheesecake, poundcake, cherries, bananas, Mandarin oranges, pretzels, apples, raspberries, brownies, beignets, graham crackers and pears.

(Use only perfect and fresh fruits. No frozen fruit allowed! Cheesecake and poundcake should not be dipped with a fondue fork, but chocolate can be poured over them. Cut bananas just before serving to prevent mushy browning.)

Fill the bottom of a fondue pot or double boiler with one inch of water. In a top liner (big enough to hold all chocolate sauce ingredients) pour in milk and turn burner to medium high. Be careful not to let the milk scorch.

Break the chocolate into small pieces. When milk becomes warm, add in half of the chocolate pieces. Stir continuously. As chocolate mixture thickens, add more of the chocolate until you have reached desired consistency.

Turn burner to low. Add marshmallow cream, but do not stir. Just before serving, add the Bacardi rum. Carefully light the chocolate sauce with a long match. While flame is still burning, stir the marshmallow cream to allow it to toast. Garnish with crushed Oreo cookies.

Mr. Fish
Seafood Market, Grill, Raw Bar
& Sushi Palace

919 Broadway Avenue
Myrtle Beach
(843) 448-6526

Mr. Fish is about as local and unpretentious as it gets. What you see is what you get: Fresh seafood, cooked right in front of you, any way you like it. You can have it fried, grilled, sautéed, jerked, blackened or steamed. If you don't want your fish cooked at all, Mr. Fish has a full sushi bar. You'll eat off of Styrofoam plates with plastic cutlery and a paper towel, but you'll eat well!

This small, storefront diner is the seat of knowledge when it comes to area seafood. Until the late '70s, Mr. Fish was the only seafood market in Myrtle Beach and continues to retail, wholesale, cut and process fish to the public and for about 100 Grand Strand restaurants. One never needs to question the quality of seafood at this establishment, since Mr. Fish must adhere to strict federal regulations from the point a fish is taken from a boat until it is handed over to a customer.

Mr. Fish is definitely the place to explore the denizens of the deep. Trust the staff's suggestions. Wade your tastebuds through unknown waters and try the Alligator Sirloin when it's on special or sample the rangoon of cream cheese and fresh crab held hot and tight in a crispy wonton wrapper.

Mr. Fish's Killer Tuna Eggroll

This recipe is a local favorite of Mr. Fish frequenters. It's piping hot when served. The veggies inside go through a steaming process during deep frying; when you open up this eggroll, your senses come alive with a pungent waft of cooked cabbage and fresh ginger.

1	head of cabbage, shredded
2	carrots, shredded
1	bunch of green onions, chopped fine
1	tuna steak
1	package of eggroll skins
2	tablespoons soy sauce
1	teaspoon sesame oil
½	teaspoon Chinese 5 spice powder
½	teaspoon white pepper

Teriyaki sauce
Fresh ginger

Lightly steam the shredded and diced vegetables until al dente. Chop the tuna steak into bite-sized pieces and sauté in teriyaki sauce. Mix cooked vegetables and tuna together and press out liquid through a sieve or colander. Add all of the seasonings, grating the fresh ginger to taste, and mix well.

Put enough of the mixture on an eggroll skin to fill it up and roll tightly. Deep fry to a golden brown. Cut the tuna roll into four pieces and serve with the dipping sauce (recipe follows). Makes 10 eggrolls.

Dipping Sauce

2	ounces white vinegar
1	ounce soy sauce
6	tablespoons sugar
1	teaspoon sesame oil
1	ounce dark mushroom sauce
1	clove of fresh garlic, minced

Fresh grated ginger to taste

Mix all of the ingredients together in a small saucepan and heat. Serve warm.

Honey Barbecue Salmon

  1 salmon filet
  3 teaspoons honey
  2 cloves of garlic, chopped
  ½ teaspoon soy sauce
  ½ teaspoon white vinegar
  ½ teaspoon lemon juice
  Fresh grated ginger to taste

Grill the salmon filet until done without any seasonings. Mix all other ingredients together in a bowl and pour over the salmon. You may heat the barbecue sauce or use it at room temperature. Makes 1 portion.

Mr. Fish's Original Lemon Fish

  1 filet of any whitefish such as flounder, grouper, cape capensis, orange roughy, rockfish or snapper
  1 container of frozen, fresh lemonade
  2 ounces white vinegar
  4 tablespoons cornstarch
  Sugar to taste
  Lemon wedges and parsley to garnish

Mix the lemonade concentrate with water and pour into a small cooking pot. Add the cornstarch and vinegar and mix in sugar in small amounts to taste. Heat long enough for the mixture to bubble and then remove from the stove and let it cool. Grill, broil or sauté the fish until done to your liking. Pour sauce over the fish and garnish with lemon wedges and fresh parsley. Makes 1 portion.

NASCAR Cafe

1808 21st Avenue North
Myrtle Beach
(843) 946-7223

Roaring into town in January 1997, NASCAR Cafe stirs together a car racing theme with dining with an interactive NASCAR museum. Eating at this cafe is a thunderous experience. Engines boom and sputter as you're suddenly surrounded by the sights and sounds of a day at the track from sky-high TV monitors that wrap around the restaurant.

The NASCAR museum is a separate, wide hallway that runs the circumference of the cafe. Objects and people of historical interest to auto racing and show cars are on display along with racing simulators and a Winston Cup retail shop.

Waiters and waitresses are referred to as "drivers" and complete the sporting ambience dressed in red, pit-crew overalls. The NASCAR menu is hefty, with most items designed to satisfy a gnawing hunger. Besides the recipes that NASCAR offered for "More Flavors of Myrtle Beach," it serves up a mean 14-ounce pork chop and a large portion of chicken that has been slow-roasted and then grilled. Coupled with broad green beans flavored with bacon and sweet potato casserole, you'll feel no hunger pangs for hours.

Grilled Chicken Pasta

This delightful spin on pasta Alfredo combines the popular creamy and cheesy sauce with the flavorful bites of red onion and sugar snap peas. This recipe is sure to be a hit with guests. Serve it at your next dinner party with toasted garlic bread.

- 2 ounces margarine
- ½ cup mushrooms, sliced
- 2 tablespoons red onion, diced
- 2 tablespoons green onion, diced
- ½ cup tomatoes, diced
- 1 pound boneless, skinless chicken breasts, cooked and diced
- 1 cup sugar snap peas
- 16 ounces Alfredo sauce
- 1 pound linguine
- 2 tablespoons Parmesan cheese, grated

Cook linguine noodles in boiling water for 8 to 10 minutes or until desired tenderness. Drain and place in a large serving dish. Set aside.

Sauté mushrooms and onions in margarine over medium heat until soft. Add tomatoes, chicken, snap peas and Alfredo sauce. Simmer on medium heat, stirring constantly, for 3 to 5 minutes or until thickened.

Top pasta with the sauce and vegetables. Sprinkle with Parmesan cheese and serve immediately. Makes 4 servings.

Grilled Chicken Salad

- 8 cups mixed salad greens
- 4 ounces herbed vinaigrette dressing (recipe follows)
- ½ cup red onions, diced
- ½ cup cucumbers, diced
- 1 cup rice noodles
- ½ cup feta cheese, crumbled
- ½ cup black olives, sliced
- ½ cup tomatoes, diced
- 1 pound boneless, skinless chicken breast, cooked and diced

In a large mixing bowl, toss together all ingredients except chicken, tomatoes and 2 ounces of the dressing.

Place salad in serving dishes and then top with chicken. Sprinkle tomatoes evenly over each salad plate. Top each with the remaining vinaigrette dressing. Serve immediately. Makes 4 salads.

Herbed Vinaigrette Dressing

2	tablespoons olive oil
1	teaspoon alma stabilizer or gelatin
½	cup water
¼	cup red wine vinegar
1½	tablespoons spicy mustard
1	tablespoon honey
2	teaspoons lemon juice
2	teaspoons black pepper
1	teaspoon salt
1	teaspoon leaf oregano
1	tablespoon fresh basil, chopped
2	teaspoons granulated garlic
½	cup olive oil
¾	cup canola oil

In a mixing bowl, add the alma stabilizer (available in specialty food shops) or gelatin with 2 tablespoons of olive oil and whip by hand until dissolved.

Add water. Using a mixer with a wire attachment, mix on low speed for 7 minutes until thick. Then pour in the vinegar and increase mixer speed to medium and mix until smooth.

Next, add in all other ingredients, except the oils, and continue mixing for 3 minutes. At a steady rate, add the olive oil and then the canola oil.

Place in a container and store at room temperature. This recipe yields 1 pint.

Official All Star Cafe

2925 Hollywood Drive
Myrtle Beach
(843) 916-8326

The day after golf prodigy Tiger Woods won the 1997 Masters tournament, he was here in Myrtle Beach at the grand opening of this Official All Star Cafe! Sharing ownership with Wayne Gretzky, Shaquille O'Neal, Ken Griffey Jr., Monica Seles, Joe Montana and Andre Agassi, All Star is a sports emporium second to none.

Twelve 8-foot television screens surround the restaurant broadcasting major sporting events, while monitors give updates and final scores for games being played around the world. As you sit in leather-like booths, fashioned like baseball gloves, a fascinating array of sports memorabilia surrounds you. There's even a Tiger Woods Clubhouse featuring items that track the star's amateur and professional days.

Food at All Star is American diner fare, stealing from the Midwestern larder of comfort vittles. Redskin potatoes are pan fried with sautéed bell peppers and red onions and can be smothered with country gravy. The prime rib sandwich is served on grilled sourdough hearth bread and a garlicky cream sauce is the base for hale and hearty pasta dishes.

Buffalo Chicken Sandwich

1	cup flour
1	tablespoon salt
1	teaspoon ground black pepper
1	cup buttermilk
1	egg
4	boneless, skinless chicken breasts
1	cup Frank's Original Hot Sauce
1	stick unsalted butter, cut into cubes

Combine the flour, salt and pepper in a bowl. In another bowl, combine the buttermilk and egg and whisk together. Dredge each chicken breast in the flour, shake off the excess, and then place in the buttermilk and egg mixture. Place the chicken back in the flour and set aside.

In a deep fryer, heat oil to approximately 350 degrees. Place each coated chicken breast in the oil and cook until golden brown (about 4 to 5 minutes), turning if necessary.

Place the hot sauce in a pan and bring to a boil. Remove from heat, and using a food processor, add the butter to the heated sauce. Coat the fried chicken breast in the hot sauce and butter mixture. Place on your favorite hamburger roll. We suggest topping with shredded lettuce and your bleu cheese dressing of choice. Makes 4 sandwiches.

Penne Chicken and Broccoli

1	ounce olive oil
1	pound chicken tenders
1	medium red pepper, diced into 1/2-inch pieces
1	pound cooked penne pasta
1	bunch broccoli, cooked and cut into florets
2	cups garlic cream sauce (recipe follows)

Heat the olive oil in a frying pan and cook the chicken tenders and red peppers for approximately 4 to 5 minutes, or until done.

Combine these ingredients with the cooked penne and broccoli and garlic cream sauce. Toss together and serve immediately. Serves 4.

Garlic Cream Sauce

½	pound butter
1	tablespoon chopped garlic

½ pound flour
1 quart heavy cream
1 tablespoon grated Parmesan cheese

In a medium saucepan, melt the butter. When butter is melted add in the garlic and sauté for about 2 to 3 minutes over medium heat. When garlic is cooked, add the flour to form a roux and cook for an additional 2 to 3 minutes. Pour in the heavy cream, stirring the entire time. Cook for 6 to 7 minutes on medium-low heat, stirring frequently.

After the sauce has cooked, add the Parmesan cheese and remove from the stove. Any leftover sauce can be saved in the refrigerator and reheated later.

Chicken Quesadillas

1 pound chicken tenders
1 teaspoon chili powder
1 teaspoon cumin
1 teaspoon kosher salt
1 ounce olive oil
½ cup salsa (whatever brand you like)
¼ cup green chilies, diced
1 cup Monterey Jack and cheddar cheese, shredded
8 flour tortillas, 8 inch size
1 pound butter mixed with garlic to taste

Sprinkle the chicken tenders with the chili powder, cumin and salt. Heat the olive oil in frying pan and cook the chicken tenders until done; approximately 4 to 5 minutes. Set aside to cool.

After the chicken has cooled, cut into small strips and combine with salsa, chilies and the cheese mixture.

Place enough of the mixture on 4 flour tortillas to cover the surface, but not thickly. Melt the butter and garlic and brush onto the remaining four tortillas. Put the brushed tortillas on top of the filled ones, buttered side up.

Place in a hot cast iron skillet, on medium-high heat, buttered side down. Brush the other side now with garlic and butter. Cook on one side for approximately 2 to 3 minutes or until the tortilla is golden brown. Using a spatula, flip over and finish cooking.

Serve with your favorite salsa, guacamole and sour cream on the side. Makes quesadillas for 4.

The Old Pro's Table

**4701 U.S. 17 South
Windy Hill Section
North Myrtle Beach
(843) 272-6060**

Displaying a priceless collection of sports memorabilia that spans 500 years, The Old Pro's Table is renowned for its reverence of the game of golf and for superb cuisine.

Inside and out, Old Pro's is a step back in time. The building itself is a classic example of Lowcountry architecture, constructed from Charleston common pink brick and heart pine siding. Beams and flooring are fashioned of wood dating back to the 1880s and 1890s and the hand-blown glass window panes that look out over the tidal marsh are about the same age.

Featured in too many regional and national publications to name, Old Pro's was the first so-called "theme" restaurant along the Grand Strand and has not disappointed first-time or regular patrons for the 20 years it has been in operation.

A feast is prepared here every evening for the eyes and palate. The dining room view peeks through century-old oak trees to a natural tidal marsh. The menu tantalizes with continental fare and French and Northern Italian flairs.

If you're feeling a bit Francais, the rack of lamb crusted with macadamia nuts and fresh herbs may tempt you, complemented with a mint-scented au jus. According to chef Tyler Rice, the most popular menu items are Old Pro's crab cakes and a 20-ounce prime T-bone steak. Tyler insists that his crab cakes be made of 100 percent fresh lump crabmeat and pan sautéed only. The cakes are served on a bed of roasted red bell peppers which have been pureed and a mustard-dill sauce accompanies.

Creme Brulee

    16 egg yolks
    ⅔   cup sugar
    2   tablespoons vanilla extract
    5   cups heavy cream
    1   tablespoon Grand Marnier liqueur

Combine the egg yolks and sugar and whip until pale yellow in color. Add in the vanilla. Pour the cream into a saucepan and bring to a slow boil. Just when it begins to roil, whisk in the egg and sugar mixture. Then, mix in the Grand Marnier.

Pour into custard cups which are set in a bake tray with high sides. Pour enough boiling water into the tray to reach halfway up the cups. Bake in the water bath at 300 degrees for about 40 to 50 minutes, or until the mixture appears set. Yields 10 to 12 depending on the size of the custard cups.

Cajun Alfredo with Smoked Salmon Bits

For the Alfredo Sauce:
    1½ quarts heavy cream
    ½   quart half and half cream
    1½ pounds Parmesan cheese
    4   ounces butter
    2½ tablespoons garlic

For each dish served:
    4   ounces smoked salmon
    ½   teaspoon Cajun Blackfish Seasoning
    6   ounces linguine

Sauté garlic in butter until clear and then combine with all the Alfredo sauce ingredients. Simmer over low heat until smooth in texture. To serve, combine 6 ounces of sauce with the smoked salmon, seasoning and linguine.

New England Clam Chowder

- ¼ pound bacon, chopped
- 1 medium yellow onion, chopped
- 2½ pounds cooked potatoes, diced
- 1 can chopped sea clams
- ¼ pound butter
- ¼ pound flour
- ¾ gallon clam stock
- ½ tablespoon thyme
- 2 bay leaves
- ½ quart heavy cream
- ¼ teaspoon white pepper
- ½ teaspoon salt

In a stock pot, cook the bacon until brown. Add in the onions and cook with the bacon until translucent.

Next, add the butter and cook for 8 minutes. Put in the spices and cook for 2 minutes more. Pour in the flour and cook for 5 minutes. Add the clam stock and cook another 10 minutes. Then, stir in all the other ingredients and cook for 10 more minutes. This recipe makes 1 gallon of chowder.

The Olive Garden

1405 N. Kings Highway
Myrtle Beach
(843) 626-8856

It's warm. It's friendly. It's the place you go for heaping plates of Italian food. It's the home of unlimited soup and bowls of salad and baskets of steaming, fresh-baked garlic breadsticks. It's the Olive Garden legacy.

True to a trattoria-style eatery in Italy, meals are moderately priced and the decor lends itself to an open festival feeling. The menu blends both classic and creative Northern and Southern Italian cuisine which runs the gamut from Calamari Alla Marinara to Eggplant Parmigiana, Fettuccine Alfredo and Mediterranean style Garlic Shrimp.

The Olive Garden concept was developed by General Mills Restaurants (a division of General Mills, Inc.) which opened the pilot "Garden" in Orlando, Fla., in 1982. Needless to say, the relaxed Italian notion became enormously popular and by 1997, Olive Gardens dotted the North American map and were employing 43,000 people in the United States and Canada. A major contributor to The Olive Garden's success is the restaurant's constant innovation, bringing diners a never-ending stream of theme menus, special combination platters and "unlimited" goodies.

Capellini Pomodoro (pictured on the cover)

- 4 cloves of garlic, finely minced
- 2 pounds plum tomatoes, seeded and diced
- 1 ounce fresh basil leaves, minced
- ⅓ cup extra virgin olive oil
- 3 ounces Parmesan cheese, grated
- 12 ounces angel hair pasta, cooked
- ¼ teaspoon black pepper

Cook the pasta according to package instructions and keep warm.

Meanwhile, mince garlic and basil. Set each aside. Seed and dice tomatoes. Grate Parmesan cheese.

Heat olive oil in a large skillet over medium heat. Add garlic and cook until it turns white. Add tomatoes and pepper and heat through, stirring constantly, about 2 to 3 minutes. Tomatoes should not lose their shape. Remove from heat.

Transfer the hot, cooked pasta to a large bowl. Toss pasta gently with the tomato mixture, basil and half of the Parmesan cheese. Serve immediately and toss with the remaining cheese. Makes 1 filling dinner.

Grilled Swordfish Pomodoro (pictured on the cover)

- 4-6 ounces swordfish
- 2 lemons, one juiced and the other to squeeze over the fish

Pinch cayenne pepper
- ¼ teaspoon salt
- 1 cup extra virgin olive oil
- 2 tablespoons parsley, chopped
- 1 cup tomatoes, diced to ¼-inch pieces

McCormick garlic pepper for seasoning

Prepare a relish for this dish first by combining all of the ingredients, except the swordfish, and leave it to sit at room temperature for one hour.

Lightly season the fish with the garlic pepper. Grill the swordfish for 3 minutes on each side, squeezing half a lemon on each side. Remove from grill and place on a plate. Top with 3 tablespoons of the relish. This dish is particularly delicious when paired with the preceding, Capellini Pomodoro.

Vegetable Lasagna

½ pound (2 sticks) butter
1½ cups heavy cream
1½ cups Parmesan cheese, freshly grated
18 ½-ounce slices mozzarella cheese
100% semolina lasagna noodles
16 ounces ricotta cheese
¼ cup Romano cheese, grated
¾ cup mozzarella cheese, shredded
2 tablespoons green onion, sliced thin
2 teaspoons fresh parsley, chopped
½ teaspoon salt
⅛ teaspoon black pepper
¼ teaspoon dry basil
¼ teaspoon dry oregano
4 cups broccoli florets, trimmed to 1-inch pieces
2 cups carrots, sliced ¼-inch, then roughly chopped
4 cups mushrooms, sliced to ¼-inch pieces
2 cups red bell peppers, diced to ¼-inch pieces
1 cup green bell peppers, diced to ¼-inch pieces
1 cup yellow onion, diced to ⅛-inch pieces
2 cups zucchini, sliced to ¼-inch pieces
Spray Pam or similar product
Freshly ground white pepper to taste

Preparing the Alfredo Sauce:

Heat water to a boil in the bottom of a double boiler. Add the butter, cream and white pepper to taste to the top pot and heat until butter is completely melted. Then stir in the Parmesan cheese until it is melted and blended. Remove the top pot and set aside to cool. Divide the sauce into 2 equal portions. Refrigerate one portion for use later.

Cooking Lasagna Strips:

Use only a good quality, 100 percent semolina lasagna, such as Creamette or DeCecco brands. Take a 9X13-inch baking pan and lay out enough dry lasagna strips to ensure you have enough to make three full layers, with very little overlap. Remove the dry strips and cook according to package directions. Drain.

Cook the noodles only until barely al dente. If pre-cooked too completely, the pasta will be too soft and lose its integrity when the assembled lasagna is baked.

Putting Together the Ricotta Cheese Mix:

Combine the ricotta cheese, Romano cheese, shredded mozzarella cheese, green onion slices, fresh parsley, salt, pepper, basil and oregano in a bowl. Add in 1¼ cups of cooled Alfredo Sauce. Blend thoroughly with a rubber spatula.

Set aside at room temperature while vegetables are being prepared.

Vegetable Mix Preparation:

Wash and drain the broccoli florets, carrots, mushrooms, red and green bell peppers, yellow onion and zucchini. Peel the carrots.

Cut the vegetables to the approximate dimensions specified in the ingredients list. If cut too large, the vegetables won't cover the layers well.

Combine all finished vegetables and mix together.

Assembly of Lasagna:

Coat the bottom and walls of a 9X13-inch baking dish with Pam or butter, margarine or oil. Lay out cooked lasagna strips (about 4) to cover the entire bottom of the dish.

Spread 1¼ cups of the ricotta cheese mix evenly over the lasagna strips. Top the ricotta cheese mix with 8 cups of vegetables and spread out evenly. Lay out 9 of the mozzarella cheese slices to cover the layer of vegetable mix.

Repeat this layering – lasagna noodles, ricotta cheese, vegetables, 9 mozzarella slices. Top the second layer of mozzarella cheese slices with lasagna strips and spread them evenly with 1¼ cups of ricotta cheese mix to finish.

Spray a sheet of aluminum foil with Pam or similar product and cover the baking dish tightly with the foil, sprayed side down. Bake in a 375-degree oven for about an hour or until the internal temperature is 165 degrees.

Remove from the oven and allow to sit for a few minutes, covered, before cutting and serving.

Immediately prior to serving, heat the reserved portion of Alfredo Sauce and ladle over each slice of lasagna. Serves 8.

The Parson's Table

U.S. 17 North and McCorsley Avenue
Little River
(843) 249-3702

The Parson's Table takes fine dining to a state of heavenly reverence, in more ways than one. The building itself was constructed in 1885 to serve as the Little River Methodist Church for this tiny fishing village. Converted into a restaurant 19 years ago, The Parson's Table still seems to echo a hymn or two, graced by majestic stained glass windows throughout.

It has been rated a five-diamond establishment and one of the top 50 overall restaurants in the United States by The Academy Awards of the dining industry. Executive chef Ed Murray Jr. has been voted the No. 1 chef on the Grand Strand by Resort Publications.

Haute cuisine is the mainstay at The Parson's Table with a menu that covers fresh local seafood, aged choice beef, veal, poultry and imaginative pasta dishes. For those with a taste for game, roast duckling sporting a raspberry demi-glace is a house favorite. And most patrons can hardly bear to leave without sampling one of the Parson's luscious desserts, any more than they can walk by the rose and herb gardens without stopping to take in the exquisite aroma.

Blackened Grouper with Kiwi-Vidalia Onion Chutney

2	cups balsamic vinegar
1	pound light brown sugar
2	teaspoons kosher salt
2	teaspoons fresh ginger, chopped
¼	teaspoon cayenne pepper
2	cups Granny Smith apples, peeled and diced
1	cup Vidalia onion, sliced thin
1	cup dried apricots, chopped
1	lemon, halved and sliced thin
3	cups kiwi fruit, peeled and chopped
4	8-ounce grouper filets
4	ounces blackening spice
½	cup olive oil

Combine the first 5 ingredients in a medium saucepan. Cook over medium heat and reduce to half. Add the apples, onions, apricots and lemon and cook for another 15 minutes. Stir in the kiwi fruit and then remove from heat. This chutney can be served at room temperature or chilled.

To prepare the grouper, heat the olive oil in a large cast iron skillet until it starts to smoke. Dredge the fish in the blackening spice and carefully place it in the hot oil. Cook on each side for 3 to 5 minutes. If your grouper is rather thick and is not done to your liking at this point, you may finish cooking it by placing the skillet in a 350-degree oven. Serve the grouper on a bed of chutney. Makes 4 dinners.

Nancy Murray's Chocolate Pecan Pie

3	cups granulated sugar
¾	cup flour
6	eggs, lightly beaten
12	ounces butter, melted and then allowed to cool
3	tablespoons vanilla
1½	cups mini chocolate chips
1½	cups white chocolate chips
3	cups pecans, chopped
2	unbaked pie shells

Vanilla ice cream

Mix the sugar and flour together. Add in the rest of the ingredients and mix well. Pour this mixture into the unbaked pie shells. Bake for one hour at 325 degrees. Remove the pies from the oven and allow to cool. Refrigerate overnight.

Heat each serving in a microwave oven for 30 to 45 seconds. Serve with a big dollop of vanilla ice cream. Makes 2 pies.

Parson's Table House Vinaigrette
    1   cup red wine vinegar
    2½ cups virgin olive oil
    1   tablespoon garlic, chopped
    1   tablespoon oregano
    1   tablespoon basil
    1   tablespoon grain mustard
    ½   cup granulated sugar
    1   teaspoon kosher salt
    1   teaspoon black pepper

Mix all ingredients well and pour into an airtight jar. Refrigerate for 24 hours.

Shake well before serving. Makes 1 quart.

NORTHERN
ITALIAN CUISINE

Piccolino's

2903 N. Kings Highway
Myrtle Beach
(843) 626-4464

The Grand Strand was introduced to the distinctive taste of Northern Italian cuisine five years ago, when Adrian Bokinac opened Piccolino's. Bokinac is both owner and chef of the establishment, bringing years of experience he gleaned with a previously owned restaurant in Long Island, New York.

Crisply clad in white shirts and black trousers, the all-male waitstaff at Piccolino's seems to forever move at a nearly frantic pace of efficiency, while Bokinac is a blur in the kitchen as he prepares and oversees every dish that is served.

Northern Italian food puts emphasis on brown sauces rather than the more familiar, red tomato base of other regional Italian cooking. A Piccolino's specialty is the Filet Mignon Barollo, where the fine cut of meat is sautéed with a touch of garlic and wine sauce. A taste for seafood may well attract you to the Salmon Dijonnaise, a broiled filet dressed with a tangy mustard spread.

Rolle Di Filetto

1	pound beef filet
2	tablespoons olive oil
1	sprig of rosemary
2	bay leaves
½	lemon, sliced
3	tablespoons butter
1	teaspoon all-purpose flour
1	cup dry white wine

Salt and fresh ground pepper to taste

Season the filet to taste with salt and pepper and place in a heavy saucepan with the olive oil, rosemary, bay leaves and lemon. Cover and cook over moderate heat for about 30 minutes, turning frequently.

Remove the lemon slices, rosemary sprig and bay leaves. Add in the butter and the flour, mixed with a few tablespoons of cold water. Pour the white wine over the meat and bring to a boil, stirring constantly.

Spoon out meat and keep it in a warm place. Reduce the sauce in the pan by stirring over high heat for a few minutes. Cut the filet into thick slices and serve in its own gravy.

Olive Al Forno

(Baked Olives)

36	large green olives, pitted
36	thin slices pancetta
2	ounces olive oil

Wrap each olive in a slice of pancetta. Thread the olives onto cocktail sticks in pairs. Place on a lightly oiled cookie sheet and bake in a moderate oven until the pancetta fat starts to melt.

Take out and place briefly on paper towels to absorb the hot fat. Serve on a warm plate.

Zabaione Caldo

½	cup sugar
4	egg yolks
1	cup sweet Marsala wine
1	lemon peel, grated
1	pinch ground cinnamon
3	drops vanilla extract

Put the sugar and egg yolks in a deep metal bowl and beat vigorously with a whisk until light and frothy. Add in the Marsala wine, lemon, cinnamon and vanilla.

Place the bowl over a saucepan of hot, but not boiling, water on low heat. Continue to beat until the mixture is fluffy. Remove from the heat and stir. Serve in a cocktail or champagne glass.

Planet Hollywood

2915 Hollywood Drive
Myrtle Beach
(843) 448-7827

Inspired by the worlds of film and television, this 43rd Planet Hollywood opened in Myrtle Beach in November 1996. The star-studded shareholder list includes Arnold Schwarzenegger, Bruce Willis, Whoopi Goldberg, Sylvester Stallone, Demi Moore and producer ("The Fugitive") Keith Barish. Needless to say, the Planet is home to a collection of Hollywood memorabilia that spans generations and genres of talent.

Planet Hollywood describes its menu as "California new classic cuisine" and borrows a nuance of flavor from Italian, Asian and regional American foods. Expect unusual pasta combinations, salads bordering on the exotic, vegetarian dishes and Schwarzenegger's mother's now-famous apple strudel.

This culinary tribute to "Tinsel Town" mixes dining with amusement, sightseeing and shopping. Besides items of Hollywood interest, video monitors throughout the restaurant preview trailers of soon-to-be-released movies and gift shops feature wares from hats and T-shirts to leather jackets.

Planet Hollywood's Chicken Crunch

This CAP'N CRUNCH-inspired style of chicken fingers is a real hit. You won't find a more satisfying or fun way to chomp on chicken.

2 cups CAP'N CRUNCH cereal
1½ cups corn flakes
1 egg
1 cup milk
1 cup all-purpose flour
1 teaspoon onion powder
1 teaspoon garlic powder
½ teaspoon black pepper
2 pounds chicken tenders or fresh chicken cut into 1-ounce strips
Vegetable oil for frying

Coarsely grind or crush both cereals together and set aside. Whisk egg and milk together in a bowl. Stir flour and seasonings together in another bowl.

Dip chicken pieces into the flour and lightly coat. Take the chicken from the flour and pull through the egg wash. Then roll the chicken in the cereal mix, coating well.

Heat the vegetable oil in a large heavy skillet or deep fryer to 325 degrees. Drop coated chicken tenders carefully into the hot oil and cook for about 3 minutes or until golden brown. Drain and serve immediately with Creole mustard sauce (recipe to follow). Makes 8 servings.

Note: Because of the sugar content in the cereal it is important not to fry above 325 degrees.

Creole Mustard Sauce

1 cup mayonnaise
¼ cup Creole-style or Dijon mustard
1 tablespoon yellow mustard
1 tablespoon horseradish
½ teaspoon cider vinegar
Dash Worcestershire sauce
1 teaspoon red wine vinegar
1 teaspoon water
½ teaspoon cayenne pepper
½ teaspoon salt
1 tablespoon green onion, sliced into ¼-inch pieces
1 tablespoon crushed garlic, packed in oil
1 teaspoon green pepper, finely chopped

1   teaspoon celery, finely chopped
1   teaspoon onion, finely chopped

Mix all ingredients together thoroughly. Makes about 1½ cups of sauce.

Spinach & Mushroom Dip

4   ounces onions, chopped
½   pound mushrooms, sliced
¼   pound butter
1   cup mozzarella cheese, shredded
¾   cup Parmesan cheese, grated
2   tablespoons lemon juice
1   tablespoon salt
1   cup sour cream
2   pounds fresh spinach blanched in water
1   quart garlic cream (recipe follows)

Sauté onions and mushrooms in butter until soft. Set aside and let cool.

Add in the mozzarella and Parmesan cheese, lemon juice, salt and sour cream to the cooled mushroom and onion mixture.

Mix together the blanched spinach and garlic cream. In a suitable container, combine all of the ingredients, cover and refrigerate. This dip can be served hot or cold. Makes ½ gallon.

Garlic Cream

1   tablespoon fresh garlic, chopped
3   ounces butter
3   ounces flour
1   quart heavy whipping cream
¼   cup Parmesan cheese, grated
Salt and pepper to taste

In a saucepan over medium heat, sauté the garlic, salt and pepper just until the garlic is cooked but not burnt. Add in the butter and flour and stir together until reaching a pasty roux.

Add in the whipping cream and bring to a boil. Whisk frequently. When the mixture comes to a boil, pour in the grated cheese and cook until blended.

Transfer to a storage container and refrigerate.

River Room Restaurant

801 Front Street
Georgetown
(843) 527-4110

Perched along the waterfront in the center of Georgetown's historic downtown, the River Room was originally a grocery store built in the 1800s. Once a bustling area of commerce, rice planters and antebellum life, the newly renovated main street of Georgetown is a dreamy hint of gracious days gone by.

In keeping with the fact that most of the world's wealthiest rice plantations were well-tended in this area during the 1850s, the River Room stays in step with local tradition by selecting its stone-ground grits from Johnsonville, S.C., and lump crabmeat from the neighboring town of McClellanville.

Like the easy, flowing waters that are the viewpoint from the restaurant's dining room, chef Joe O'Hara prefers to run his kitchen with consistency and an eye for presentation, rather than speed.

The River Room specializes in chargrilled fish – caught locally, of course – which is kissed by a flavor only an open flame can produce.

What would O'Hara suggest the perfect River Room meal to be? The appetizer of choice should be the shrimp and grits with chunks of sausage and a hint of ham. Chargrilled grouper is his definite entree of preference and dessert must be the pound cake. Homemade lemon zest pound cake is prepared every day, sautéed in clarified butter and set adrift on a pool of dark caramel sauce. The luscious concoction is topped off with ice cream and fresh fruit.

Herb Encrusted Grouper

4   8-ounce grouper filets
2   cups Progresso breadcrumbs
2   tablespoons fresh basil, chopped
2   tablespoons fresh cilantro, chopped
2   tablespoons fresh parsley, chopped
Olive oil for sautéing
Salt and pepper to taste

Preheat oven to 350 degrees.

Mix breadcrumbs with the fresh herbs and salt and pepper in a bowl. Brush the filets with a little of the olive oil

In an oven-proof skillet, over medium high heat, heat olive oil until hot. Dredge the grouper filets in the crumb and herb mixture and cook on one side until golden brown, then turn the filets over and place the whole pan in the oven for about 17 minutes to finish cooking. Serve with lemon slices and butter. Makes 2 dinners.

Black Bean Soup

1   pound dry black beans that have been soaked overnight in water
2   smoked ham hocks
1   large onion, chopped finely
4   celery stalks, chopped finely
2   chicken bouillon cubes
Salt and pepper to taste

In a stock pot, place beans, ham hocks, onion, celery, salt and pepper. Mix bouillon cubes in water to make enough to cover the bean mixture.

Cook the beans over medium heat until they become soft. When soft, carefully put the beans in a food processor and puree to a soup consistency. If you do not have a food processor, a hand held mixer works just as well.

You can keep the soup warm in a pot on low heat, stirring often. Garnish with chopped tomatoes and sour cream.

New Orleans Bread Pudding with Bourbon Sauce

3   eggs
1¼ cups sugar
1½ teaspoons vanilla extract
1¼ teaspoons ground nutmeg
1¼ teaspoons ground cinnamon
¼   cup unsalted butter, melted
2   cups milk
½   cup raisins
½   cup pecans, coarsely chopped
French bread cut into 1-inch cubes, enough to fill a brownie pan to the top

With a mixer, beat eggs in a bowl on high until extremely frothy and bubbles are the size of pinheads; about 4 minutes. Add in the sugar, vanilla, nutmeg, cinnamon and butter. Beat on high until well blended. Then, beat in the milk. Stir in the raisins and pecans.

Grease a brownie pan and fill with the cubes of bread. Pour egg mixture over the bread, making sure to evenly distribute the raisins and pecans. Let the pan of ingredients sit for at least 30 minutes, occasionally patting down the bread into the liquid to totally soak it.

Bake at 350 degrees for 35 to 45 minutes.

Bourbon Sauce

½   cup butter
1½ cups powdered sugar
2   egg yolks
½   cup bourbon

Melt the butter and sugar over medium heat until all of the butter is absorbed. Remove from the heat and blend in the egg yolks. Pour in the bourbon, a little at a time, until you reach the desired taste, stirring constantly. Sauce will thicken as it cools. Pour over a serving of bread pudding.

ROSSI'S

Rossi's Italian Restaurant

9636 N. Kings Highway
Galleria Shopping Center
Restaurant Row
Myrtle Beach
(843) 449-0481

When Deane Morris, Jack Patterson and James Karahalios got together to start a restaurant, they put to the test a combination of too-many-years-to-count experience and time-honored family recipes. The ensuing result was Rossi's Italian Restaurant, where diners bring a hearty appetite and throw all vestiges of dieting out the window.

Chef Brad Brookshire prides himself in consistent quality. Rossi's features homemade, old-style sauces – lots of butter and cream, the way mama used to make it. And, just the way mama intended, no one leaves Rossi's tables hungry.

A lot of pasta anchors plates or is served as an accompaniment to many entrees. Even the delectable Tuna A La Rossi – a grilled or blackened tuna with cilantro-lime beurre blanc – is delicately placed over a bed of angel hair pasta.

Rossi's is well-known for its combination plates that incorporate meat with seafood. A favorite example is the veal ribeye stuffed with spinach, Portabello mushrooms and mozzarella cheese and topped off with a veal demi-glace. The veal is happily coupled with a serving of shrimp scampi. To fully complement every meal, Rossi's tenders an extensive wine list.

Grouper Parmigiana

1	8-ounce grouper filet
1	tablespoon onion, minced
1	ounce lemon juice
6	ounces butter
2	ounces Parmesan cheese, grated
2	ounces white wine
1	egg yolk
6	ounces salad oil
½	teaspoon dried mint
½	teaspoon dried basil
½	teaspoon dried oregano
1	ounce red wine vinegar

Salt and pepper to taste

Prepare a dressing by whipping the egg yolk, red wine vinegar, mint, basil and oregano together in a bowl. Slowly pour in the salad oil. Season with salt and pepper. Set aside.

Make a lemon butter sauce by melting the butter and adding in the lemon juice. Set aside.

Place the grouper on a broiler pan and top with the minced onion. Then, add the wine and one ounce of the lemon butter sauce. Broil the filet in the oven until it is half cooked, about 4 minutes. Take the fish out of the oven and pour the prepared dressing over top. Follow with the grated Parmesan cheese and slightly pack it down. Broil again until golden brown and serve it with the remaining lemon butter. Makes 1 portion.

Oysters Rockefeller

6	oysters on the half-shell
1	ounce melted butter
1	ounce onion, minced
8	ounces chopped spinach
1½	ounces Sambuca
3	slices bacon, baked and crumbled

Hollandaise Sauce (recipe to follow)

Sauté onions in the butter in a saucepan. Add in the spinach and Sambuca. When spinach is cooked, remove from the stove and allow to cool. Then place the spinach mixture on top of the raw oysters and place in the oven for about 5 minutes. Top with Hollandaise Sauce (recipe to follow) and crumbled bacon.

Hollandaise Sauce

1 ounce apple cider vinegar
1 teaspoon Tabasco sauce
2 ounces water
4 egg yolks
12 ounces clarified butter
1 tablespoon lemon juice

Add all ingredients together, except the butter. Whip in a double boiler until the yolks ribbon. Gradually add the clarified butter while constantly whisking. Add the lemon juice last and season with salt and pepper if you wish.

Sam Snead's Grille

9708 N. Kings Highway
Restaurant Row
Myrtle Beach
(843) 497-0580

For the Epicurean and golf enthusiast, Sam Snead's is the perfect place to mix dining pleasure with a fascinating tribute to one of golf's greatest legends. This namesake restaurant features a massive collection of memorabilia from Snead's illustrious PGA career, made even more impressive by the surroundings of polished woods and softly spilling light.

A delightful, smoky ambience at Sam Snead's is created by the signature cooking method of grilling foods over pecan and oak. Snead's is the culinary home of oak-smoked ribs with a Jim Beam barbecue sauce and a wood-burning oven where pork chops, fresh seafood and beef are uniquely prepared.

Sam Snead's is a place to visit for dinner when you're good and hungry with enough time to peruse a golf collector's treasure trove.

Roasted Red Pepper Salsa

½ tablespoon crushed red pepper
1 fresh jalapeno pepper
2 tomatoes
½ green pepper
½ yellow pepper
½ red pepper
½ yellow onion
3 tablespoons fresh cilantro
1 jar Old El Paso Salsa (Green Chili style)
2 tablespoons garlic salt
¼ cup jalapeno juice
3 tablespoons salad oil
3½ tablespoons Durkee hot sauce
Salt to taste

Remove seeds from all halves of peppers. Place peppers in a bowl with the salad oil and coat well. Remove the peppers and shake off the excess oil. Place the oiled peppers on a baking sheet and broil until they are at least 50% blackened. Remove from broiler and allow to cool.

Hand cut the onions, cooled peppers and tomatoes to a ½-inch dice. Cut the jalapeno peppers to a ¼-inch dice.

Place the diced vegetables plus the cilantro in a bowl and add the garlic salt, jalapeno juice, salsa, salt to taste and crushed red pepper. Mix well.

Place in a closed container and refrigerate for at least 12 hours. This recipe makes 1 quart.

Smoked Shrimp Bisque

10 ounces butter
8 ounces flour
1 ounce shallots, chopped
3 tablespoons tomato paste
½ tablespoon paprika
¼ teaspoon chopped garlic
¼ teaspoon cayenne pepper
6 quarts half and half cream
2 quarts heavy cream

10	ounces shrimp base
2	ounce dry vermouth
1	ounce dry sherry
2	pounds shrimp, chopped
1	pound smoked Gouda cheese, shredded
1	teaspoon wild rice, cooked per bowl

Melt butter and add flour to a stock pot, blending well. Cook for 2 minutes over medium heat.

To the butter and flour mixture, add in the shallots, tomato paste, paprika, garlic and cayenne pepper. Cook for 2 minutes.

Add in the half and half and heavy cream, slowly bringing the pot to a boil. When boiling, put in the shrimp base, vermouth, sherry and chopped shrimp and cook until the shellfish is done. Add the shredded gouda and cook until the cheese is completely melted.

Put the wild rice at the bottom of each soup bowl or cup and ladle in the bisque to serve. Makes 2½ gallons.

Carolina Marinade

3	teaspoons dry basil
¾	teaspoon crushed peppercorns
¼	tablespoon garlic, diced
1½	cups soy sauce
1	cup red wine vinegar
1½	teaspoons crushed red pepper
1½	cups fresh ginger, chopped
12	tablespoons honey
3	cups sesame oil
½	cup fresh lime juice

Mix all ingredients together, cover in a container and refrigerate. Use as a marinade for fish and shellfish. Makes 1 gallon.

Sante Fe Station

1101 U.S. 17 North
North Myrtle Beach
(843) 249-3463

A 15-year-old landmark of North Myrtle Beach, Sante Fe Station is true to its name, being built around authentic railroad cars. Just as train travelers were once treated to fine meals in dining cars, Sante Fe offers diners one of the largest menus in the area in a leisurely atmosphere.

The extensive bar and lounge is known locally for fun happy hours and daily food and drink specials. Give yourself time to adequately read Sante Fe's menu, which will remind you of a city telephone directory, and expect generous portions of whatever you select.

Locally owned and operated, Sante Fe is usually involved with community causes and activities throughout the year and prides itself on consistent efforts to accommodate each customer's individual needs and preferences when it comes to cooking styles or recipe ingredients.

Key Lime Pie

> 5 egg yolks
> 1 can sweetened condensed milk
> 2 ounces Rose's Lime Juice
> 1 graham cracker pie crust

Place egg yolks in a bowl and beat with a wire whisk. Add in the sweetened condensed milk, a little at a time, mixing thoroughly. Pour in the lime juice and blend well.

Pour mixture into the pie crust and place in a 350-degree oven for approximately 10 minutes or until the filling is set. Remove from the oven and refrigerate. Top with whipped cream if you like. Makes 1 pie.

Sante Fe Crab Cakes

> 5 pounds backfin crabmeat, shells removed
> 1 small onion, diced
> 5 eggs
> 5 tablespoons mayonnaise
> 1 tablespoon parsley flakes
> 1 tablespoon Old Bay seasoning
> 1 tablespoon prepared mustard
> Cracker meal for breading

Mix first seven ingredients together and portion into 5-ounce patties. Roll in cracker meal and deep fry at 350 degrees until golden brown.

Serve with a side of mustard sauce if you prefer. Makes 16 crab cakes.

Chicken Quesadilla

2	10-inch flour tortillas
¼	cup vidalia onion, diced
¼	cup purple onion, diced
¼	cup sweet red pepper, diced
¼	cup green bell pepper, diced
¼	cup mushrooms, sliced
½	cup mix of Monterey Jack and cheddar cheeses, shredded
2	boneless, skinless chicken breasts

Olive oil for sautéing
Taco seasoning to taste
Sour cream and salsa as sides

Julienne the vegetables and chicken and sauté in olive oil with the taco seasoning to taste until all ingredients are cooked. Place the mixture between the two tortillas and add the shredded cheese.

Place on a pizza pan and put into a 350-degree oven to bake until all of the cheese is melted. Remove from oven and serve with sour cream and salsa on the side for dipping. Makes 1 quesadilla.

Sea Captain's House

3000 N. Ocean Boulevard
Myrtle Beach
(843) 448-8082

A spectacular panoramic view of the Atlantic Ocean is the perfect complement to a sumptuous seafood meal at Sea Captain's House.

The restaurant's building was originally a private beach cottage, built in 1930. It was converted into a guest house (The Howard Manor) in 1954 and finally became the Sea Captain's House in 1963. Family owned and operated since its inception, Sea Captain's House prides itself in its exceptional staff and serving high-quality dishes.

Seventy-five percent of cuisine served here is seafood – all fresh and carefully selected. Chef Tom Mullally says that he comes to work every day with the express intention of "wowing" his diners. Mullally cites freshness and variety as Sea Captain's claim to 35 years of fame – he even personally tends to the fresh herb garden cultivated across the street from the restaurant.

Mullally trained in culinary arts in Switzerland for four years and claims that "you do this work because it's something you truly love." Best known for his signature sauces, the chef has developed such seafood favorites as a fresh tangerine and basil sauce for salmon, and bacon shrimp hollandaise to top grouper. Mullally regularly delights patrons with his specials, including a homemade seafood lasagna (pasta made from scratch) and hand-rolled shrimp ravioli.

Crab Cakes with Lemon Dill Butter Sauce (pictured on the cover)

Rather than fried, these crab cakes are lightly sautéed, allowing them to drink up the mild beurre blanc-style sauce. Prepare yourself for a taste sensation from one of the most popular kitchens in town.

2 pounds high quality lump crabmeat, picked of any shell
1 small onion, diced
1½ cups packed, fresh breadcrumbs
2 tablespoons fresh chopped parsley
3 eggs, beaten
¾ teaspoon salt
1 teaspoon black pepper
1 teaspoon dry mustard
¼ cup heavy cream
1 teaspoon cooking oil, butter or margarine
Flour

To a hot skillet, add the cooking oil, butter or margarine and diced onion. Sauté until the onion is transparent; approximately 3 minutes. Remove from heat.

In a large mixing bowl, combine all the rest of the ingredients. Mix them together well. Form the mixture into 3-ounce cakes (about 3 inches across). Roll the cakes in enough flour to cover and then cook in hot oil until golden brown on both sides. Serve immediately with lemon dill sauce (recipe follows). Makes 16 crab cakes; 8 dinner portions.

Lemon Dill Butter Sauce (pictured on the cover)

1 stick unsalted butter (¼ pound), cut into 1-inch squares
2 teaspoons fresh lemon juice
2 tablespoons white wine
1 teaspoon dried dillweed or use 2 teaspoons of fresh, minced dillweed
Salt and pepper to taste

In a saucepan over medium heat, pour in wine and add butter, stirring to blend. Add lemon juice, dillweed, salt and pepper to taste. Serve immediately.

Shrimp Salad (pictured on the cover)

2 pounds medium shrimp, boiled, peeled and deveined
¾ cup mayonnaise
½ cup diced green bell pepper
½ cup diced celery
½ cup sweet salad cubes
¼ cup capers
Juice of half a lemon
Salt and pepper to taste

Mix all ingredients together in a bowl and enjoy! Serves 4.

She Crab Soup

2 large onions, fully diced
1 cup clarified butter
2 cups all-purpose flour
2½ quarts half and half cream
1 quart heavy cream
1½ teaspoons ground mace
1 cup good quality sherry
1 pound fresh white crabmeat (must be good quality)
Salt and pepper to taste

In a large stockpot, cook onions in butter until soft. Add flour, reduce heat to low, stirring constantly for 15 minutes.

Add milk products and continue stirring. Add remaining ingredients and simmer for 30 minutes, stirring frequently. Makes 1 gallon.

T-Bonz Gill & Grill

4732 U.S. 17 South
Barefoot Landing
North Myrtle Beach
(843) 272-7111

21st Avenue North & U.S. 17 Bypass
Myrtle Beach
(843) 946-7111

Two Grand Strand locations of T-Bonz Gill & Grill fill empty tummies with the heartiest portions of beef, grilled chicken, seafood and vegetarian entrees. Of course, beef of all shapes and cuts is T-Bonz's biggest seller When it comes to red meats, chef Bobby Hubbard makes sure that it's done big and it's done right.

To accompany all meals, this restaurant carries a larger-than-usual selection of imported and domestic wines and beer. Perhaps this is the reason that T-Bonz is always buzzing with lively chatter and the atmosphere seems almost buoyant.

T-Bonz made its mark on the local map very early by practicing overt measures to be environmentally conscious. All plastics, glass and cardboard materials used at T-Bonz are recycled. The use of Styrofoam is strictly avoided. And, from the kitchen point of view, no food preservatives, additives, flavor enhancers or MSG's are used in food preparation. So, you can be sure that you'll be leaving T-Bonz with your thirst quenched and your appetite satisfied.

Market Street Chicken and Shrimp

4-6 chicken breasts
1-2 cups white select shrimp (depending on your taste)
1   4-ounce can chipotle peppers in adobo sauce
1   quart heavy cream
2   ounces flour
2   ounces butter
Dash Tabasco sauce for color

Make a roux in a saucepan with the flour and butter, stirring constantly. Add in the peppers and cream and simmer until thick. Give the sauce a dash of Tabasco.

Grill the chicken breasts to desired doneness. Sauté the shrimp just until pink.

Place the cooked shrimp over each chicken breast and pour the jalapeno cream sauce over. Makes 4 to 6 servings.

Drunken Ribeye

4-6 ribeye steaks
4   ounces horseradish sauce
2   cups olive oil
2   cups water
4   ounces teriyaki sauce
1   onion, sliced
1   ounce ginger
2   ounces cracked black peppercorns
4   ounces molasses
1   pint beer
1   cup bourbon
Salt to taste

Blend all of the ingredients together. Place the ribeye steaks in this marinade for at least 36 hours. Cook the marinated meat to taste. Makes 4 to 6 portions.

Grouper Deluxe

4-6 grouper filets
1-2 cups white select shrimp (depending on your taste)
2   cups Chardonnay wine
2   cups heavy cream
⅛ cup freeze dried shallots
1   tablespoon honey
Pinch of salt
⅛ teaspoon pepper
2   ounces flour
2   ounces butter

Bring the shallots and wine to a boil in a saucepan and cook until reduced by half. Add in the heavy cream and cook until reduced by half, again. Stir in the honey, salt and pepper.

Meanwhile make a roux with the flour and butter in a pan over medium heat, stirring constantly.

Reduce the heat under the cream sauce. Add in the roux and simmer over low heat until thick.

Grill the grouper filets for 6 minutes on each side. Sauté the shrimp just until it turns pink.

Place the shrimp over each grouper filet and pour the creamy Chardonnay sauce over it to serve. Makes 4 to 6 dinners.

BROOKGREEN
Gardens

The Terrace Café at Brookgreen Gardens

1931 Brookgreen Gardens Drive
Murrells Inlet
(843) 237-4218

Sitting amid a renowned botanical and sculpture garden, The Terrace Café evolved from a mere snack stand that served guests a small bite and beverage to tide them over. In the spring of 1996, the snack shop received a major face lift and renovated interior, reopening as a full-service restaurant with a new Lowcountry menu.

Historical Brookgreen Gardens is the site of a former plantation, rich in history, and its home cafe features dishes in keeping with that heritage. The Terrace caters to regional tastes, with such favorites as barbecue and cole slaw, red rice and sausage, shrimp and grits, chicken pilau and red velvet cake.

From March through December, the Café staff serves within the gardens. In the spring and summer months, visitors can sip a cool, refreshing beverage and have a light repast in the Old Kitchen Garden. Warm cups of tea and hot cider is the fare during the chillier months of fall and winter. You never know – at Brookgreen Gardens you may end up sharing a snack or two with an inquisitive deer.

Cheese Biscuits

8   cups self-rising flour
2   cups butter-flavored Crisco
1   tablespoon baking powder
3   cups buttermilk
2½ cups cheddar cheese, grated
1   teaspoon red pepper

Blend flour, baking powder, pepper and Crisco until crumbly. Add cheese. Pour in buttermilk and knead together. Roll out and cut into biscuits. Bake for 12 to 15 minutes at 350 degrees.

She Crab Soup

½   stick margarine
½   cup flour
1   quart half and half cream
2   cups milk
1½ cups crabmeat
¼   teaspoon salt
¼   teaspoon nutmeg
¼   teaspoon white pepper
½   teaspoon onion powder
1   teaspoon Worcestershire sauce
Dash of sherry for each serving

Melt margarine in a heavy-bottomed pan and add in flour, mixing well. Cook to make a roux, stirring with a plastic spoon for 5 minutes.

Gradually add the half and half while stirring constantly. Mix in the salt, nutmeg, pepper, onion powder and Worcestershire sauce. Whip with a wire whisk to incorporate all the spices.

Cook on low heat until the soup has thickened. While the soup is thickening, pick through the crabmeat to remove the cartilage. Add the crabmeat to the soup. Serve each bowl with a dash of sherry.

Marinated Salad

1   head broccoli, chopped
1   head cauliflower, chopped
1   large onion, diced
1   can artichokes
1   can red pimento
1   cup olives, sliced
1   cup stuffed olives, sliced
1   large green pepper, cut into rings
1   small jar pickled cherry tomatoes
½   cup red wine vinegar
1   teaspoon thyme
½   cup sugar
½   cup salad oil
Salt and pepper to taste

Mix all of the vegetables together in a large bowl. Prepare the dressing by mixing together the red wine vinegar, thyme, sugar, salad oil and salt and pepper in a container with a lid. Shake vigorously and pour over the vegetables. Refrigerate.

Shrimp and Grits Casserole with She Crab Sauce

Casserole:
1   cup grits, cooked
6   eggs, beaten
2   cups half and half cream
2   cups grated cheddar cheese
½   teaspoon red pepper
½   teaspoon thyme

She Crab Sauce:
2   cups She Crab Soup
1   teaspoon white pepper
1   teaspoon Worcestershire sauce
1   teaspoon onion powder
½   teaspoon Old Bay spice
½   teaspoon nutmeg
½   teaspoon red pepper
8   shrimp, cooked for each serving

Mix all of the casserole ingredients together in an appropriate baking dish and put into a 250-degree oven for 30 minutes. Cool and cut into squares.

Blend all of the sauce ingredients together. Place 8 shrimp on top of a casserole slice and pour the she crab sauce over top.

Chicken Pilau

1	large roasting chicken
1½	cups smoked sausage
2	celery stalks, chopped
1	onion, chopped fine
1	teaspoon chicken base
½	teaspoon pepper
1	teaspoon salt
1	cup rice for every 2 cups of stock made

Cook chicken, salt, pepper, base, onion and pepper together until tender. Skin and debone chicken. Measure the stock and use one cup of rice for every 2 cups of stock.

Put chicken and its stock, rice and sausage in a heavy pot and bring to a boil. Boil for 3 minutes and then simmer for 40 minutes.

Lady Fingers

½	cup margarine
1¼	tablespoons powdered sugar
1	cup finely chopped nuts
1	cup flour
1	teaspoon vanilla

Mix all the ingredients until it forms a soft dough. Roll the dough until it is the size of your smallest finger. Cut the roll into 2-inch pieces. Bake at 325 degrees until light brown. Cool and roll in the extra powdered sugar.

Red Velvet Cake

Cake:

½   pound Crisco
1½ cups sugar
2   eggs
1   tablespoon vinegar
1   cup buttermilk
2½ cups flour
¼   teaspoon red food coloring
2   tablespoons cocoa
1   teaspoon vanilla
1   teaspoon baking soda
1   teaspoon salt

Cream the Crisco and sugar. Add eggs. Make a paste using the cocoa and food coloring and add to sugar mixture. Combine the salt and vanilla with the buttermilk and slowly add this in along with the flour. Mix in the baking soda last. Pour into a cake pan and bake at 325 degrees for 20 to 25 minutes.

Icing:

1   egg
½   stick margarine
1   box powdered sugar
2   teaspoons vanilla
1   cup chopped nuts

Cream together the egg, margarine, sugar, vanilla and ½ cup of the chopped nuts. Ice the cake when it's cool and sprinkle the remaining nuts over the top.

Thoroughbreds Restaurant

9706 N. Kings Highway
Restaurant Row
Myrtle Beach
(843) 497-2636

Although eating at Thoroughbreds may seem like acceptance into an exclusive country club, it will feel more like dining in someone's well-appointed drawing room.

A 1996 reader poll conducted by The Sun News found this restaurant to be the "most romantic" along the Grand Strand. Consistently outstanding food and service has earned Thoroughbreds a AAA, 3-Diamond rating.

Continental cuisine is served in four beautiful and intimate dining rooms. Tableside dishes such as Caesar Salad, Steak Diane and Bananas Foster are favorites among regular patrons.

The recipe for success at Thoroughbreds is painstaking, yet simple: consistent high quality, innovative nightly specials, a highly trained staff and a plush interior decor.

Grilled Portabello Mushrooms (pictured on the cover)

1	pound fresh Portabello mushrooms
1	cup olive oil
⅛	cup garlic cloves, minced
1	tablespoon fresh basil, chopped
2	tablespoons fresh parsley, chopped
1	lemon, juiced

Whisk all of the ingredients together (except the mushrooms) and leave at room temperature overnight.

Slice the mushrooms about a half-inch thick. Submerge the pieces in the marinade mixture. Allow them to sit for at least 2 minutes to soak up the flavor.

Grill the mushrooms at medium heat on a flat or charcoal grill until tender.

Perfect Duckling

2	ducklings
1	tablespoon honey
2	tablespoons soy sauce
2	gallons plus ¾ cup water
4	ounces fruit preserves
4	ounces red wine

Place ducklings on a steam rack and trim excess fat around the neck and cavity areas. Remove the giblets. Using a fork, prick the skin.

Place the ducks over 2 gallons of boiling water. Cover and steam for one hour. After an hour, remove the cover and let ducklings cool slightly.

Combine the honey, soy sauce and ¾ of a cup of water. Brush the mixture over the ducks, making sure to cover all sides.

Place in a 425-degree oven for approximately 15 minutes, rotating once during cooking or until brown on all sides.

While browning the meat, remove the fat from the steaming broth and boil to reduce to one pint. Add in the red wine and preserves and reduce until thickened. Season sauce with salt and sugar if desired and serve on the side. Carve the duck much like a chicken or turkey. Serves 4.

French Onion Soup (pictured on the cover)

1	pound onions
1	ounce cooking oil
2	ounces sherry wine
2	ounces Marsala wine
1	quart chicken stock
1	quart beef stock
½	bay leaf
4	⅛-inch slices provolone cheese
4	½-inch slices Italian bread

Pinch of black pepper

Heat oil in a small pot and add onions. Lightly brown the onions and cook until soft. Add the wines and reduce until the alcohol burns off. Put all remaining ingredients, except the cheese and bread, in the pot and bring to a boil. Taste and adjust salt to your liking.

When the soup is made, pour into 4, 12-ounce crocks. Place bread and cheese on top of crocks and broil in the oven until golden brown. Makes 4 servings.

Kentucky Jim Beam Rack of Lamb

1	lamb rack, frenched per serving
2	ounces breadcrumbs
2	teaspoons brown sugar
1	teaspoon chopped pecans
3	ounces Jim Beam bourbon
1	egg
2	ounces brown sauce
3	ounces heavy cream

Flour for dredging

Combine breadcrumbs, 1 ounce of the bourbon, 1 teaspoon of the brown sugar and pecans.

Bread lamb by rinsing, pat dry and place in flour, egg and breadcrumb mixture; in that order.

Roast in a 350-degree oven until desired doneness is achieved. While cooking lamb, mix together remaining 2 ounces of bourbon and 1 teaspoon of brown sugar with brown sauce and cream. Reduce until the mixture coats the back of a spoon.

Pour sauce over lamb to serve.

Tyler's Cove Restaurant

Hammock Shops
Pawleys Island
(843) 237-4848

Nestled among the quaint Hammock Shops of Pawleys Island, azaleas and old oaks weeping Spanish moss, Tyler's Cove was built on the site of the native Waverly Plantation.

Although it has a casual ambience, the Cove could rival many of America's loveliest inns, complete with an old-fashioned tap room. Exposed, antique brick floors and walls make their historic mark on the atmosphere and solid oak ceiling beams at Tyler's were borrowed from area antebellum homes.

Tyler's menu is a taste of the real South with exciting entrees like pork medallions sautéed in Applejack Brandy, applebutter and cream, served with garlic smashed (that's mashed in Southern) potatoes; roasted quail with pistachio stuffing and a honey-thyme sauce or Bourbon Shrimp heaped top Carolina cheese grits. Yum-yum, y'all.

Pumpkin and Shrimp Soup

1	cup celery, chopped
1	cup onion, chopped
1	carrot, chopped
1	red pepper, diced small
1	tablespoon olive oil
½	teaspoon thyme
1	teaspoon celery salt
1	teaspoon white pepper
¼	teaspoon mace
¼	teaspoon nutmeg
½	teaspoon cinnamon
½	teaspoon salt
½	cup dry sherry
1	pound small shrimp, cleaned
2	cans pureed pumpkin (Libby's is best)
1	quart water
1	teaspoon chicken base or 1 bouillon cube
3	quarts heavy cream or half and half

Cook the first 4 vegetables in the olive oil in a stock pot until transparent; about 8 to 10 minutes. While the vegetables are sautéing, add in the 7 spices and stir to blend well.

Pour in the sherry to deglaze the pot and add in the cleaned shrimp. Sauté shrimp until done.

Create a paste by mixing in the pumpkin. Next, pour in the water and stir to loosen all the ingredients. Add the chicken base and heavy cream. Heat until the soup simmers and adjust spices to taste. Makes 1 gallon.

Monkfish Medallions

4	pieces (¾ to 1 pound) cleaned monkfish
	Seasoned flour for coating
	Olive oil to coat pan
¾	cup mushrooms, sliced
3	scallions, chopped
1	tablespoon shallots, chopped
1	tablespoon butter
½	cup sherry

125

Salt, pepper and parsley to taste
Toast points (slice of toast cut into 4 triangles)

Dredge fish in seasoned flour. Heat pan and add oil. When the oil is hot, add the fish; cook on one side and then flip to cook the other side.

Add in the vegetables and sauté for 3 minutes. Salt and pepper to taste. Pour in the sherry and stir gently. When the sherry coats everything, add the butter and melt.

Remove the fish to a plate, placed on top of toast points. Stir sauce and pour over fish. Sprinkle with parsley. Serves 2.

Broccoli Salad

2   pounds broccoli florets, washed and drained
½   cup bacon bits
½   cup mozzarella cheese
1½ cups mayonnaise
½   cup sugar
¼   cup red wine vinegar

In one bowl, mix together the first 3 ingredients. In another bowl, mix the next 3 ingredients until the consistency is smooth. Toss both mixtures together.

Villa Mare

7819 N. Kings Highway
Northwoods Plaza
Myrtle Beach
(843) 449-8654

Unless you're a sub sandwich shop or an all-you-can-eat Chinese buffet spot, it's usually difficult to stay in the restaurant business in a strip mall location. But, Villa Mare has maintained brisk traffic since opening its quaint bistro eight years ago in the Northwoods Plaza. Locals quickly sniffed out Villa Mare, with their keen sense for good value.

Its formula for prosperity is simple, but one that takes incredible determination and endurance. Villa Mare is family owned and operated, spanking clean and serves only high-quality, fresh, made-to-order Italian food. Yes, you'll wait a little longer for your specialty spinach and mushroom pizza or plate of white seafood pasta, but Fred Fusco will serve no pre-fabricated dish to his customers.

Since you'll never get bad eats at Villa Mare, the "Medley Platters" have become best sellers since they offer you a variety of tastes and eliminate the pressure of menu selection. Trio medleys include veal scaloppini, fettuccine Alfredo and chicken piccata or a combination of veal and chicken Marsala with fettuccine Alfredo. The "duo" platter is made up of chicken parmigiana and stuffed manicotti.

Breaded Artichoke Appetizer

2	artichoke hearts, cut in half

Flour
Breadcrumbs

4	eggs
1	cup Parmesan cheese
1	cup olive oil

Lemon wedge
Salt and pepper to taste

Make an egg batter by whisking together the eggs and Parmesan cheese.

Dip the artichoke halves in flour, then in the egg batter, and then in breadcrumbs.

Pan fry the breaded artichokes in the olive oil on each side until they're golden brown. Season to taste and serve with a lemon wedge. Makes 1 portion.

Veal Marsala

2	ounces veal, pounded

Flour

¾	cup fresh mushrooms, sliced
4	ounces olive oil
4	ounces sweet Marsala wine
4	ounces veal stock
1	ounce chicken stock

Salt and pepper to taste

Cut the pounded veal into 4 medallions and lightly flour.

Sauté the veal and mushrooms together in hot olive oil. Add salt and pepper to taste. Pour in the Marsala wine and allow the alcohol to burn off. Finally, add in the veal and chicken stocks and continue cooking until the broth has reduced by one-third. Serve immediately. Makes 1 serving.

Chicken Florentine

 5 ounces fresh spinach (stemless)
 1 boneless, skinless chicken breast, pounded
 5 ounces olive oil
Flour
 1 cup white wine
 ½ lemon
 2 tablespoons Parmesan cheese
 2 slices provolone cheese
 1 tablespoon granulated garlic
Salt and pepper to taste

Sauté fresh spinach in one ounce of the olive oil with the granulated garlic and Parmesan cheese. Salt and pepper to taste.

Next, sauté the chicken breast in the remaining 4 ounces of olive oil, adding in the wine and lemon when the chicken becomes golden brown in color (add the lemon only after the alcohol has cooked out of the pan).

To serve, place the cooked chicken breast on a dish and cover it with the sautéed spinach. Then cover the spinach with the provolone slices and pour the sauce from the pan over the whole plate. Yields 1 portion.

Wishbones
at Wild Wing Plantation

1000 Wild Wing Boulevard
Conway
(843) 347-1900

Wishbones has the distinction of being the home restaurant of a beautiful, 33,000-square-foot clubhouse serving the Wild Wing Plantation golf courses. Entirely enclosed by glass, the view from any table at Wishbones is a tranquil panorama of the gently rolling fairways and grassy knolls of the Hummingbird course. Other Wild Wing courses include the Wood Stork, Avocet and Falcon championship courses.

Chef Roger Miller comes to Wishbones with a degree from the Culinary Institute of America in Hyde Park, New York. Miller specializes in our regional, Lowcountry cuisine and is a master mixer of sauces, soups and homemade desserts. In fact, his 1997 submission into the "Taste of Conway" festival won Wishbones the Best Dessert of the Show award.

From fresh local seafood dishes to deli-style sandwiches, Wishbones has become a favorite lunch spot for locals and has hosted its fair share of receptions, formal dinners and corporate meetings. The facility is always excited to share its list of international buffets available to groups which includes menus representing Hawaii, Scandinavia, South Africa, Australia and Ireland.

Sauté Chicken Dijon

1   7-ounce boneless, skinless chicken breast
2   cups chicken stock
1   bay leaf
3   cups heavy cream
5   tablespoons Dijon mustard
6   tablespoons Parmesan cheese
3   ounces butter
3   ounces flour
Flour for dredging
Butter or Pam cooking spray for sautéing

Place the bay leaf in the chicken stock and bring to a boil in a pot. Make a roux with the butter and flour, mixing together until thickened. Slowly add the roux to the boiling chicken stock. Simmer on low heat for 10 minutes. Slowly add in the rest of the ingredients, except the chicken, and cook over low heat for another 10 minutes. Strain and return to the pot to simmer on low heat.

Lightly bread chicken breast in flour. Sauté in a hot pan with butter or Pam. Cook thoroughly, browning both sides of the chicken. Place the chicken breast on a serving plate and ladle the Dijon sauce over top. Makes 1 serving.

Chocolate Layered Grand Marnier Cheesecake Topped with Chocolate Ganache

4   ounces unsweetened chocolate
1   cup milk
1¼ cups cake flour
2½ teaspoons salt
4   egg yolks, beaten
2   cups confectioners' sugar
1   teaspoon vanilla
4   egg whites, beaten
1   tablespoon baking powder

To make sponge cake: Sift cake flour with baking powder and salt and set aside. Melt chocolate and milk in a pan. In another bowl, cream the 4 beaten egg yolks and sugar. Gradually add in the chocolate mixture and then the flour mixture. Then fold in the beaten egg whites. Pour into cake pan and bake in a 350-degree oven for 50 minutes.

4   egg yolks, beaten
¾   cup sugar
¼   teaspoon salt
⅓   cup milk
2   tablespoons gelatin

131

¼ cup water
1½ teaspoons vanilla
1½ pounds soft cream cheese
4 egg whites
½ cup sugar
1 cup whipping cream
1 tablespoon Grand Marnier liqueur
1 pound chocolate chips
1 cup heavy cream
Toasted almonds

To make gelatin cheesecake: Using a double boiler, beat eggs, sugar, salt and milk until thickened. Soak gelatin in water and then add to warm egg mixture until it dissolves. Let cool, then add vanilla.

Beat cream cheese until smooth, then gradually add in egg mixture. In another pan, beat the egg whites and the sugar until stiff. Fold into the cream cheese mixture, followed by the whipping cream and the Grand Marnier. Let set until slightly firm.

Once cake is done, remove from the pan. When cake is cool, slice horizontally into 3 disks. Spread cheesecake mixture between layers and stack. To make ganache, melt chocolate chips over double boiler, add the cream and stir until smooth. Pour over cake while ganache is still warm. Refrigerate at least 2 hours before serving.

Apricot Stuffed Porkloin

1 boneless whole center cut porkloin
5 cups apricots in heavy syrup
2 tablespoons cinnamon
½ teaspoon nutmeg
1 cup honey
5 ounces brandy
Salt and pepper to taste

Taking a boning knife, insert the blade in the end of the porkloin, lengthwise. Be sure to keep the blade in the middle of the pork. Cut one inch through the loin.

Drain syrup off the apricots. Marinate the apricots in the brandy, cinnamon, nutmeg and honey for 15 minutes.

Using a pastry bag, pipe the marinade mixture into the cut made in the porkloin. Place in a roasting pan with a little water in the bottom. Cover the pork with the remaining apricot mixture.

Roast in a 350-degree oven for 1½ hours. Remove the porkloin from the pan and let sit for 15 minutes. Deglaze the pan over hot heat with water. Use the glaze to top each slice of porkloin.

Yamato Steakhouse of Japan

1213 Celebrity Circle
Broadway at the Beach
Myrtle Beach
(843) 448-1959

Being a hibachi-style Japanese restaurant, Yamato Steakhouse is one place where you will always encounter at least eight Teipan chefs at one time, in full view as they prepare your food. A sizzling hotplate sits at the center of every table and the expert chefs dazzle their dining patrons with rapidly flashing knives, flying shrimp tails that land atop their tall hats and sleights of hand.

A full complement of food is served with every Yamato order that begins with salad and soup, followed by cooked vegetables, heaps of rice and finally, the main entree. It is a rarity that anyone ever leaves Yamato's yearning for more food.

In a separate section, a full sushi bar offers a wide array of tasty morsels, including the familiar raw varieties to tempura delights. It is a show of skill and mastery just to watch the sushi chef prepare the intricate menu items.

Filet Mignon and Shrimp for Two

16 ounces filet mignon
16 ounces 13/35-count shrimp
Vegetable oil for cooking
Butter for cooking
½ fresh lemon
Soy sauce to taste

Lightly oil a pan or hotplate with vegetable oil and drop in butter to taste. Mix in enough soy sauce to make the cooking base brown or to taste.

Cut the filet mignon into bite-sized portions and cut off the tails from the shrimp. Cook the meat first, stirring until desired doneness. Then, place the shrimp in the pan or hotplate and squeeze the lemon over them. Shrimp should be cooked when they turn pink and begin to curl.

Index of Recipes

APPETIZERS

BEEF

BREADS

CASSEROLES

CHICKEN

DIPS

DRINKS

DUCK

FISH AND SEAFOOD

FONDUE

LAMB

PASTA

Location of Restaurants

Myrtle Beach

1. Austin's At The Beach
   2606 N. Kings Highway

2. Benito's Brick Oven and
   Ristorante Italiano
   1308 Celebrity Circle
   Broadway at the Beach

3. The Bistro
   5101 N. Kings Highway

4. Collectors Cafe
   7726 N. Kings Highway

5. Croissants Bakery & Cafe
   504-A 27th Avenue North

6. Fusco's Restaurant
   5308 N. Ocean Boulevard
   Beach Colony Resort

7. Giovanni's
   504 27th Avenue North

8. Hard Rock Cafe
   1322 Celebrity Circle
   Broadway At The Beach

9. The Library
   1212 N. Kings Highway

10. Littles At The Beach
    411 79th Avenue North

11. Magoo's Fine Food,
    Sports & Spirits
    905 Oak Street

12. The Melting Pot
    5001 N. Kings Highway

13. Mr. Fish Seafood Market,
    Grill, Raw Bar & Sushi Palace
    919 Broadway Avenue

14. NASCAR Cafe
    1808 21st Avenue North

15. Official All Star Cafe
    2925 Hollywood Drive

16. The Olive Garden
    1405 N. Kings Highway

17. Piccolino's
    2903 N. Kings Highway

18. Planet Hollywood
    2915 Hollywood Drive

19. Rossi's Italian
    Restaurant
    9636 N. Kings Highway
    Restaurant Row

20. Sam Snead's Grille
    9708 N. Kings Highway

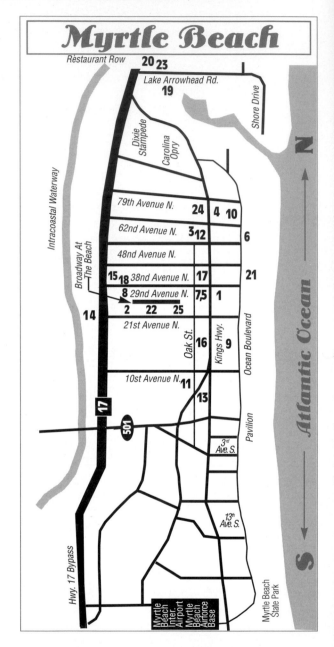

Restaurant Row

21. Sea Captain's House
    3000 N. Ocean Boulevard

22. T-Bonz Gill & Grill
    21st Ave. N. & U.S. 17 Bypass

23. Thoroughbreds
    Restaurant
    9706 N. Kings Highway
    Restaurant Row

24. Villa Mare
    7819 N. Kings Highway

25. Yamato
    1213 Celebrity Circle
    Broadway at the Beach

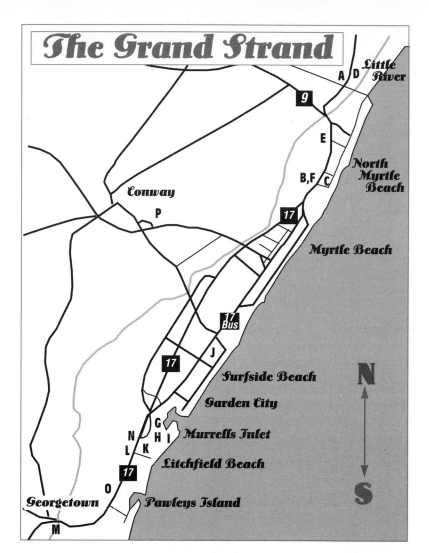

The Grand Strand

North Strand

A. **Cappuccino's**
1535 U.S. 17 North
Little River

B. **House of Blues**
4640 U.S. 17 South
Barefoot Landing
North Myrtle Beach

C. **The Old Pro's Table**
4701 U.S. 17 South
North Myrtle Beach

D. **The Parson's Table**
U.S. 17 N. & McCorsley Ave.
Little River

E. **Sante Fe Station**
1101 U.S. 17 North
North Myrtle Beach

F. **T-Bonz Gill & Grill**
4732 U.S. 17 South
Barefoot Landing
North Myrtle Beach

South Strand

G. **Anchovies Restaurant**
4079 U.S. 17 Business
Murrells Inlet

H. **Bovine's**
U.S. 17 Business South
Murrells Inlet

I. **Capt. Dave's Dockside**
4037 U.S. 17 Business
Murrells Inlet

J. **The Charleston Cafe**
815 Surfside Drive
Surfside Beach

K. **Drunken Jack's**
4031 U.S. 17 Business
Murrells Inlet

L. **The Mayor's House**
2614 U.S. 17 South
Litchfield Beach

M. **River Room Restaurant**
801 Front Street
Georgetown

N. **The Terrace Cafe at Brookgreen Gardens**
1931 Brookgreen Gardens Dr.
Murrells Inlet

O. **Tyler's Cove Restaurant**
Hammock Shops
Pawleys Island

Conway

P. **Wishbones at Wild Wing**
1000 Wild Wing Boulevard
Conway

Glossary of Terms

Al Dente

To the bite. Refers to pasta and vegetables cooked only until firm, not soft or overdone.

Clarified butter

Butter that has been heated to separate the impurities. The top layer is mostly used for cooking. It is clearer in color, but less flavorful. Also called drawn butter.

Crouton

A small piece of bread or dough, usually toasted or baked.

Cut in

To mix articles together with two knives or a pastry blender.

Deglaze

To dissolve sediment left in a pan with wine, stock or other liquid.

Demi-glace

Brown sauce reduced by half, nearly to a glaze state.

Flambe

French word for flamed. Usually refers to food that is ignited with small amount of heated liquor, the burning alcohol causing flames.

Grits

Corn kernels with bran and germ removed by crushing and sifting. A Southern favorite, usually served in a porridge form.

Phyllo

Very thin sheets of dough, layered and filled with food. The word means "leaf".

Roe

Eggs from fish or shellfish.

Roux

A mixture of flour and butter or fat in equal proportions, cooked slowly. It is used to thicken sauces and soups.

Sauté

To cook food quickly in some sort of fat, stirring to brown evenly.

Zest

The outer colored skin of citrus fruits where essential oils are concentrated.

MORE FLAVORS OF MYRTLE BEACH ORDER FORM

Please mail me _____ copies of "More Flavors of Myrtle Beach" at $12.95 (includes postage/handling). S.C. residents add 50¢ for sales tax. Canada residents add $1 for postage.

Name _____

Address _____

City/State/Zip _____

Phone _____

Check Enclosed ❏   Visa ❏   MC ❏   AmExp ❏

Credit Card # _____

Signature _____ Exp. Date _____

Make checks payable to The Sun News and mail to The Sun News,
Attn: Cashier, P.O. Box 406, Myrtle Beach, S.C. 29578

MORE FLAVORS OF MYRTLE BEACH ORDER FORM

Please mail me _____ copies of "More Flavors of Myrtle Beach" at $12.95 (includes postage/handling). S.C. residents add 50¢ for sales tax. Canada residents add $1 for postage.

Name _____

Address _____

City/State/Zip _____

Phone _____

Check Enclosed ❏   Visa ❏   MC ❏   AmExp ❏

Credit Card # _____

Signature _____ Exp. Date _____

Make checks payable to The Sun News and mail to The Sun News,
Attn: Cashier, P.O. Box 406, Myrtle Beach, S.C. 29578

MORE FLAVORS OF MYRTLE BEACH ORDER FORM

Please mail me _____ copies of "More Flavors of Myrtle Beach" at $12.95 (includes postage/handling). S.C. residents add 50¢ for sales tax. Canada residents add $1 for postage.

Name _____

Address _____

City/State/Zip _____

Phone _____

Check Enclosed ❏   Visa ❏   MC ❏   AmExp ❏

Credit Card # _____

Signature _____ Exp. Date _____

Make checks payable to The Sun News and mail to The Sun News,
Attn: Cashier, P.O. Box 406, Myrtle Beach, S.C. 29578

Notes